EDITOR: M,

OSPREY
MILITARY

ELITE

SOVIET BLOC
ELITE FORCES

Text by
STEVEN J ZALOGA *and* JAMES LOOP
Colour plates by
RON VOLSTAD

First published in Great Britain in 1985 by
Osprey, Publishing,
Michelin House, 81 Fulham Road,
London SW3 6RB

British Library Cataloguing in Publication Data

Zaloga, Steven J. and Loop, James
    Soviet Bloc Elite forces.—(Elite; 5)
    1. Warsaw Treaty Organisation—Armed Forces
    2. Special operations (Military science)
    I. Title   II. Series
    356'.16   UA646.8

    ISBN 0-85045-631-2

Filmset in Great Britain
Printed in Hong Kong

Artist's Note

Readers may care to note that the original paintings
from which the colour plates in this book were
prepared are available for private sale. All
reproduction copyright whatsoever is retained by the
publisher. All enquiries should be addressed to:

Model Emporium
700 North Johnson,
Suite N, El Cajon
California 92020
USA

The publishers regret that they can enter into no
correspondence upon this matter.

Acknowledgement
The authors wish to thank Will Fowler and Michael C
for their assistance during the preparation of this book

Soviet Bloc Elite Forces

Introduction

The élite forces of the Soviet Union and its Warsaw Pact allies are undoubtedly the largest in the world, and among the least known. Indeed, the Soviet élite formations alone have a total strength comparable to that of the entire British armed forces. There are extensive references to élite formations in Soviet military publications, but seldom is any detail provided on their mission or scope. The same is the case with the allied armies of the Warsaw Pact. The aim of this book is to provide a general review of these enigmatic troops through an examination of their historical roots, current organisation, equipment, uniforms and probable missions. (Due to the sensitive nature of this subject there are, nevertheless, units which cannot be covered in this book.)

The élite forces of the Soviet Union and the Warsaw Pact differ from their Western counterparts in a number of respects. Besides the conventional military élite formations such as airborne and marine forces, most Warsaw Pact armies have special, 'political' élite formations which are used for internal security. These are not merely police formations, but have a distinct and important military rôle in time of war: units like the KGB's Border Guards have seen combat more often since 1945 than nearly any other Soviet military formation. Therefore, while the main focus of this book will be on the more conventional élite formations, some attention will be paid to these often ignored security units.

Soviet Elite Forces

The Armed Forces of the Soviet Union (VS-SSSR) are organised into services which differ from the normal European or American practice. The VS-SSSR has four main elements: the Soviet Army, the Soviet Navy, the KGB's Border Guards and the

A paratrooper radio operator of the Soviet VDV photographed during the 'Zapad-81' exercises on Poland's western border in 1981. Note the blank-firing device on the muzzle of his AKSD; and the late-model BMD-1M in the background, identified by the 30 mm turret gun in place of the standard 73 mm weapon. (Sovfoto)

Interior Army of the MVD. The Soviet Army is the predominant force and consists of the Strategic Rocket Forces (RVSN), the Ground Forces (SV), the Air Forces (VVS), and the Air Defence Forces (PVO). The largest of the Soviet élite organisations is undoubtedly the airborne force, which forms a semi-autonomous branch of the VS-SSSR known as the VDV (*Vozdushno-Desantnaya Voyska*: the Air Assault Force). The Soviet Army refers to its marines as the Naval Infantry (*Morskaya Pyekhota*) and they are an integral part of the Soviet Navy (VMF).

Soviet paratroopers prepare their BMD-1M airborne combat vehicle for operations shortly after an air drop during the 1984 'Shield' exercise in Czechoslovakia. The *desantnik* nearest the camera is armed with the new AKR, a short carbine version of the AKSD for vehicle crews. The VDV patch worn on both sleeves of the combat overall is very evident in this view. (Sovfoto)

The VDV Airborne Forces

Of a more shadowy nature are the special troops of the GRU, which is the Intelligence service of the Armed Forces, and is an inter-service organisation somewhat akin to the American DIA. It is responsible for Intelligence troops in the various branches of the VS-SSSR, including reconnaissance and special purpose troops. The special troops of the GRU have traditionally been called *razvedchiki* (scouts) or *vysotniki* (rangers) in the Soviet Union, although these days they are popularly called *Spetsnaz* (*Spetsialnoye Naznachenie:* Special Purpose) due to their popularisation in the books of the former GRU officer who writes under the pseudonym of Viktor Suvorov. Elements of the Border Guards also warrant characterisation as élite formations as they are far more than border police. The Soviet Army also has troops known as *raydoviki* (raiders), but this term may refer to other specialist troops like the Spetsnaz rather than to a distinct element of the army.

The Soviet Armed Forces were the pioneers of paratroop and air landing forces in the late 1920s and early 1930s. Initial trials were conducted in 1930 which led to the formation of the first paratroop landing unit (PDO: *parashyutnodesantniy otryad*) in the Leningrad Military District in 1931. By 1932 four of these units had been formed; and the following year the Leningrad unit was expanded into the 3rd Special Purpose Airborne Brigade, with both paratroop and assault glider sub-units. All four units were subsequently expanded in this fashion.

Their first serious test came in the 1934 Byelorussian Military District (MD) summer manoeuvres; and they received world-wide attention in 1935 when foreign observers were invited to the 1935 Ukrainian MD exercises near Kiev, where a public drop of 2,500 paratroops was made. This was an unprecedented display of this new branch, and served as an important catalyst in inspiring interest in airborne forces elsewhere in Europe and

America. Although part of the Air Force at the time, in 1939 the 212th Airborne Brigade was deployed to the Far East, where it received its baptism of fire as ordinary infantry in the battle of Khalkin Gol against the Japanese Army. During the invasion of Poland in September 1939 the 201st, 204th and 214th Airborne Brigades were committed, but saw little if any action in an airborne rôle.

The first use of Soviet paratroopers in combat took place in 1929, when small detachments were dropped in Central Asia to combat Islamic rebels. The first full scale combat jump in history was made near Petsamo, Finland, in November 1939 by Soviet airborne troops; but this was not particularly successful, nor was a later jump against the Mannerheim line. In view of the dismal performance of regular Red Army troops, three of these élite Air Force brigades were committed to the Finnish fighting as regular infantry. They regained their wings in June 1940, when the 201st and 204th Airborne Brigades were parachuted and air-landed during the occupation of Romanian Bessarabia, with the 214th Airborne Brigade serving as a reserve.

The success of these units, and their fine combat record, led to the decision at the end of 1940 to expand the VDV to six brigades. In 1941 assessments of the German successes with airborne troops led the Soviet Armed Forces to expand the five European VDV brigades into Airborne Corps, with the sixth brigade remaining in the Far East. Each of these Corps consisted of three brigades, though by Western standards the Corps were in fact of divisional size. These units were still being formed when war broke out with Germany in June 1941, and their technical assets were completely inadequate. For example, a single one of their 16 brigades required about 120 TB-3 bomber/transports to carry out an airdrop—but the VDV never had more than 200 TB-3s available to it at any one time. Moreover, the Luftwaffe made short shrift of even this small force. Following the devastating Luftwaffe attacks on Soviet airfields in June 1941, the VDV was never able to muster more than 25 TB-3 bombers. Later, they managed to appropriate about 50 PS-84s (DC-3 copies) from the civilian Aeroflot, but each of these could carry fewer than 20 paratroopers with their gear.

This shortage of airlift meant that the VDV units spent most of the war under the control of the Red Army as normal infantry. Strangely enough, the VDV was expanded into ten Corps in September 1941, and two independent assault glider regiments were added in August 1942. In the early winter of 1942 there were several attempts to employ some of these units in the airborne rôle on the Western Front. The 201st Airborne Brigade was dropped behind German lines near Medzyn on the night of 2/3 January. The atrocious weather prevented the planned air-landing of reinforcements; and the unit had to fight its way out in blizzard conditions. It was used again in another failed drop near Vyazma on 18 January; and the 204th Airborne Brigade was dropped near Rzhev on 14–22 February to reinforce an isolated army group.

The most ambitious plan was to drop the entire 4th Airborne Corps near Vyazma behind German

Soviet paratroopers pose in front of the open clamshell doors of an Il-76 transport before a winter jump. They wear the standard Soviet Army pile cap—*ushanka*—instead of the usual winter jump helmet, perhaps because of very low temperatures. (Sovfoto)

The Soviets have pioneered the use of heavy platforms for airborne landings; these appear to be BMD platforms. Posts protrude beneath the platforms, triggering a retro-rocket to soften the impact of the main structure.

lines. In order to do this, 550–600 heavy aircraft were needed; but instead they were provided with only 22 clapped-out TB-3s and 40 Aeroflot PS-84s. In view of this lack of equipment, the plans called for the air transport regiments to fly two or three sorties every night for a week. From 27 January to 2 February about 2,100 paratroopers (a quarter of the Corps) were dropped in appalling winter conditions: the operation was a complete fiasco, and the survivors were absorbed into a neighbouring cavalry unit. The remainder of the 4th Airborne Corps was mobilised later in the month for a drop behind German lines to support a counter-offensive against Yukhnov. No additional aircraft were available, so the unit was dropped on the nights of 17/18 to 22/23 February in even worse weather conditions. The Corps was badly scattered, and fought as isolated partisan units until June, when the last isolated remnants broke out through the German lines. An operation scheduled to last three days had turned into a five-month campaign!

These heroic, slap-dash operations led the Soviet High Command to convert the Corps to Guards Rifle Divisions in 1942. They fought with distinction in the northern Caucasus and at Stalingrad. Traditions die hard, however; the Air Force managed to have them re-formed as Guards Airborne Divisions from September 1942 to February 1943, and six new divisions were added after the summer of 1943. Nevertheless, they remained as élite infantry under Red Army control. In September 1943 another major drop was planned, to parachute and air-land 10,000 troops of the 1st, 3rd and 5th Guards Airborne Brigades over the Dniepr River to secure a bridgehead. The attempt was a costly failure. By a cruel irony, the only successful airborne operation by Soviet forces in the Second World War were small-scale drops by special Naval Infantry paratroopers in the Crimea, and operations by improvised Army units during the campaign against the Japanese in Manchuria in 1945.

The VDV emerged from the war in a state of disarray. On the one hand, the VDV units had displayed exemplary courage and heroism, and some 196 'desantniki'—airborne troops—received the highest Soviet decoration, the Hero of the Soviet Union medal. Yet on the other hand nearly all major airborne operations had been badly managed fiascos. Even though the VDV was part of the Air Force, insufficient aircraft were provided, which foredoomed many of the operations. The issue of airlift would remain a pressing concern of the VDV for the next few decades.

In 1946, the VDV was transferred from the Air Force to the direct control of the Ministry of Defence to serve as a strategic reserve. Over the next decade the VDV languished, but the future rôle of the airborne divisions was examined in the light of Second World War experience. Assessments of the conduct of airborne operations by other armies were not particularly encouraging. The Soviets concluded that with the exception of the German use of paratroopers in Holland and Belgium in 1940, wartime airborne operations were either failures or had no decisive impact on the conduct of army operations. Moreover, these assessments found that airborne forces gained tactical success only when fighting against severely weakened or disheartened opponents. When facing quality units,

as in the encounter between British airborne and German armoured units at Arnhem, the results were usually catastrophic for the airborne units due to their lack of firepower.

Yet the conviction remained that an airborne force had enormous operational potential for wreaking havoc in an enemy's rear area in support of conventional mechanised forces. As a result, the VDV was retained; and efforts were initiated to circumvent the problems with airlift and firepower. In 1956 the VDV was switched to the Ground Forces and came under the control of Gen. V. F. Margelov, a wartime hero of the Soviet Naval Infantry, who would lead the VDV through its modernisation programmes over the next decades. The first substantial enhancement to the VDV came in 1955 with the first flight of the An-8 transport, which was the first modern aircraft of the VTA (Military Transport Aviation) to have any

A company of *desantniki* are inspected by their officers before a winter drop from an Il-76. They wear the padded jump helmet derived from tank crew headgear. In the background a number of D-30 122 mm howitzers are being towed to the flight line to participate in the drop. (Sovfoto)

The 103rd Guards Air Assault Div. remains the primary reserve of the 'Limited Contingent of Soviet Forces—Afghanistan', and is stationed at Bagram airfield. Here a group of *desantniki* in service uniform pose with Afghan soldiers.

served weapons, the firepower of airborne divisions was considerably enhanced by the development of special light armoured vehicles. In the early 1950s Soviet design teams worked on a lightly armoured, tracked 76 mm howitzer, the ASU-76, and a similar 57 mm gun tank destroyer, the ASU-57. The latter was accepted for quantity production and entered service in 1955, with nine in each airborne regiment. It could be carried in special P-90 parachute containers, one under each wing of a Tu-4 bomber. Later, a special heavy load platform was designed for the new An-8 transport which employed a special retro-rocket braking system. Work followed on a light airborne tank and a light airborne tank destroyer based on the PT-76 scout tank; but only the latter, designated ASU-85, was accepted for production. It entered service in 1960, and 31 serve in each airborne division's assault gun battalion. Unlike the ASU-57, it was designed primarily for air-landing from the new, larger An-12 transport. Over the next decade further improvements were made in the VDV's airlift capability and firepower. In the wake of the Cuban missile crisis embarrassment in 1963, the Politburo decided that it must significantly revamp Soviet capabilities to project its power worldwide. As a

The VDV often use the standard Soviet Army white snow camouflage overalls during winter manoeuvres, and some units are ski-qualified. (Sovfoto)

real capability to drop or land airborne forces. Prior to the arrival of the An-8, the VDV had been forced to rely on the old Li-2 (C-47 copy), supplemented by Tu-4 bombers (B-29 copies) in the cargo dropping rôle. The An-8 was followed in 1964 by the more successful An-12, which has been the backbone of the VDV's airlift to this day.

A key shortcoming in VDV firepower was the inability of its units to deal with enemy tanks. The VDV had been the world's first force to be equipped with recoilless anti-tank weapons in the mid-1930s, but these were never entirely successful. Airborne units began to receive the new B10 82 mm recoilless rifle (RCL) in the early 1950s, and this was followed later by the more potent B11 107 mm RCL which benefited from the evaluation of US RCLs captured in Korea. For short range defence against tanks, the VDV initially received a copy of the Second World War German Panzerfaust, the RPG-1, which was followed in the early 1950s by the considerably more potent RPG-2.

Crew-served weapons like RCLs were too bulky to be dropped with the paratroopers, so special containers were developed which could be dropped by even the Il-28 jet bomber. Besides these crew-

result in 1964 the VDV was again shifted back to the direct control of the Defence Ministry as a special force for the Soviet High Command.

The reorganisation of the VDV as a semi-autonomous branch of the Soviet Army marked a significant watershed in VDV history. It was shortly after this decision that two important changes began to be implemented, which have resulted in a major shift in the complexion of the VDV—changes which continue to this day. In the 1960s the Soviet Ground Forces had undergone tactical and equipment changes to permit their units to fight on a nuclear contaminated battlefield. The VDV realised that airborne divisions could be extremely useful in theatre nuclear war by exploiting the devastation created by nuclear strikes. However, their troops could not survive unprotected in the contaminated regions where they would be expected to land and operate. The VDV selected the same option as the Ground Forces' infantry units: that is, an armoured vehicle which permitted the *desantniki* to fight from within the protection of the vehicle. The VDV initiated development of a smaller, lighter version of the Ground Forces' BMP infantry combat vehicle. This emerged in 1970 as the BMD (*Boyevaya Maschina Desantnaya:* Airborne Combat Vehicle).

Jump training for the VDV includes tower jumps, and many other exercises familiar to Western paratroopers. Note that weapons are carried during training.

The BMD Airborne Combat Vehicle

The introduction of the BMD in 1970 marked the shift of the VDV from a force depending primarily on light, air-landed infantry to a mechanised air assault force with considerably more firepower. The BMD is a unique type of vehicle; no other army fields an armoured vehicle specifically designed for airborne infantry squad action. Initially, the BMDs were used to equip only one of the three regiments in each division. However, as production has continued, this has been gradually expanded to the point where all three regiments in most divisions are now fully BMD-equipped; and there are now about 320 BMDs in each division. As the BMD became available, the ASU-57 was gradually withdrawn from service.

The BMD is, in many respects, a smaller cousin of the BMP. It uses the same turret assembly, and a de-rated version of the same engine. However, the hull design and suspension are completely new. The internal configuration of the BMD differs considerably from the BMP, and is even more cramped. The hull forward of the turret contains stations for three crewmen: the squad commander to the left, the driver in the centre, and the squad machine gunner to the right. Each has his own hatch and vision periscopes; the commander and machine gunner also have firing ports from which the squad PKM or RPK can be fired. Immediately behind this forward compartment is the turret, which appears to be identical to that found on the BMP, and is crewed by a single gunner. The main 2A20 73 mm low pressure gun is automatically loaded from a revolving magazine of 40 rounds. The 9M14M Malyutka (AT-3 'Sagger') missile launcher above the main gun is manually loaded, and two 'ready' rounds are carried internally. The turret is also fitted with a co-axial PKT 7.62 mm machine gun. Behind the turret assembly is the seating for the three remaining members of the squad. On the later versions of the BMD the two squad members on either side are provided with firing ports. The engine and transmission are found in the rearmost compartment. There is a large internal fuel pannier in the right rear corner of the vehicle, supplemented on later vehicles by two small external tanks. The BMD has a variable suspension which is locked down when the vehicle is paradropped, and which can be used to lower its height during air transit. It is fully protected by chemical, atomic and biological filters: the early versions used active infra-red night sights, but more recent models have passive image intensification night sights.

The BMD is lightly armoured, although some sources indicate that its armour is heavier than that on the BMP (20 mm vs. 14 mm). Nevertheless, this is only adequate for protection against small arms fire and artillery shrapnel. It has formidable firepower, and excellent mobility; but its light weight and small size have resulted in some performance and handling constraints. The armament system shares the same shortcomings as that

The principal air defence for VDV units is the compact ZU-23 'Sergei' 23 mm twin anti-aircraft gun. Its lack of sophisticated fire controls lessens its effectiveness against high performance aircraft; but it can be a formidable weapon when used against ground targets. (Sovfoto)

on the BMP: the Malyutka missile is difficult to aim due to its primitive guidance system, especially from a moving armoured vehicle; the main 73 mm gun is short-ranged; and its finned projectile is vulnerable to cross-winds to a greater extent than more conventional ammunition. The BMD is not a particularly rugged vehicle, either, and drivers are instructed to drive with care at high speeds to prevent damage to the suspension and lower body panels.

The BMD has been plagued by many other structural shortcomings. Its fuel tank is poorly supported, and when it is partially empty the fuel tends to slosh around, loosening it from the mountings: as can be imagined, a loose and damaged fuel tank in the engine compartment can be quite dangerous. The transmission is fragile, and when shifting gears under a heavy load the shift lever sometimes pulls free from the shifting fork, leaving the transmission stuck in gear. This can be avoided by the driver lowering the engine RPMs before shifting, but this requires more driver care than is often exhibited in the field. There have also been reports that BMD drivers frequently tamper with the governor to coax a bit more speed out of the engine, which has resulted in some instances in

The SD-44 85 mm anti-tank gun is a derivative of a 1944 weapon, modified for airborne use by the addition of a small auxiliary motor which permits the gun to be driven away under its own power at low speed, eliminating the need for a towing vehicle. Like the ASU-57 just visible in the centre background, it seems to be in the process of gradual replacement by more modern weapons. (Sovfoto)

undue strain on the transmission, and burned-out clutch plates. Of more concern to the crew is the poor ventilation in the early models. Insufficient attention was paid during the design stage to the problem of venting gun fumes when the squad fires either its own weapons or the main vehicle weapons while 'buttoned up' in combat. There were some severe problems as a result: most notably, asphyxiated crews. This problem has been addressed in later models, which have improved ventilation. Yet, in spite of these shortcomings, the BMD provides the VDV with unparalleled firepower and mobility in its airborne regiments; and many of these problems have been rectified in later models.

The first version of the BMD, which appeared in 1970, would seem to have been a pre-series type which was used for initial operational testing. In 1973 an improved type appeared, the BMD-1 Model 1973. The main external change was a new circular CBR filter vent on the right side of the hull in lieu of the earlier square panel. In about 1980 the BMD-1M appeared: this was a heavily redesigned vehicle, distinguishable externally by a new style of roadwheels, and by new grill vents on the vehicle bow. Internal improvements probably took place as well. In 1981 a variant of this vehicle was shown at the 'Zapad-81' manoeuvres with a new 30 mm automatic cannon in lieu of the earlier 73 mm gun. The main attraction of such a weapon is that it offers greater accuracy and longer-ranged performance than the 73 mm low pressure gun. The most recent improvement in the vehicle's firepower was

publicly displayed for the first time in 1983. On this version of the BMD-1M, the 9M14M Malyutka has been replaced by the 9K111 Fagot (AT-4 'Spigot') anti-tank missile with its associated 9S451 launcher. The Fagot appears to be based on the Euromissile Milan, and is a considerably more accurate system than the Malyutka. However, the current fitting is of an improvised nature, and in order to fire the missile the gunner has to open the hatch and operate the launcher controls on the outside of the turret.

Besides these five variations of the BMD-1 series there are at least two support versions in use, believed to be designated as BMD-2, but known in NATO as the BMD Model 1979. These are lengthened versions of the BMD with an added road wheel on each side. The basic BMD-2 is a support vehicle and can be used to tow light weapons such as the ZU-23 anti-aircraft gun; the BMD-2KShM is a command vehicle with additional communications equipment. As in the case of the BMD-1, there are two families of the BMD-2: the initial types with the star pattern wheels, and the later types with the bow grills and sun-burst pattern wheels like the BMD-1M. The BMD is now being joined by a new airborne assault gun vehicle, possibly designated MZA, to replace the older ASU-85.

Parachute or Helicopter?

The second important change in the VDV came in 1967, when the Soviet Army began experimenting with the tactical use of helicopters. The VDV had always been envisioned as a paratroop or air-landing force. However, air-landing by aircraft implied the ability to seize an airfield in advance of the arrival of the main force. This proved practical in certain peacetime operations against erstwhile allies, like the seizure of Prague airport in the 1968 Czechoslovak invasion and Kabul airport in the 1979 Afghanistan invasion. In wartime, against a mobilised foe, the prospects for such an action are more dubious. In the 1960s the US Army demonstrated a suitable alternative in the form of the tactical employment of helicopters in this rôle, notably in Vietnam. While helicopters were hardly new to the military scene, the arrival of new models powered by the more reliable turbine engine made them more practical for this demanding rôle. In the

The ASU-85 assault gun remains in use in Soviet airborne units, though it is now being replaced. It is not designed for parachuting, and must be air-landed, in this case by An-12 transports. (Sovfoto)

Soviet Union the Mi-8 began to replace the older, bulkier Mi-4, and this permitted the formation of the first airmobile brigades in the early 1970s. The airmobile brigades are light infantry formations which do not use the BMD; but in the late 1970s air assault brigades were formed—a heavier counterpart, in which two of the four infantry battalions are equipped with BMDs. The BMDs can be carried by the Mi-6 helicopter, but units are now beginning to receive the improved Mi-26.

The VDV, since its 1964 subordination to the Ministry of Defence, has been used primarily as a strategic strike force for use in sensitive and demanding missions. In the 1968 invasion of Czechoslovakia the 103rd Air Assault Division was air-landed at Prague airport after it had been seized by a special operations team, a Spetsnaz GRU group. In 1979 the 105th Air Assault Division, supported by elements of the 103rd Air Assault Division, was air-landed at Kabul airport.

Operation 'Danube'

The plans for the invasion of Czechoslovakia in

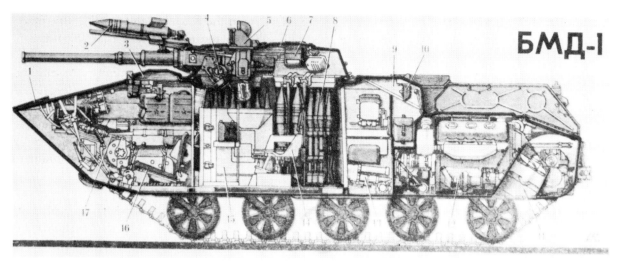

БМД-1

This Soviet illustration shows the internal configuration of the BMD-1: (1) Wave deflector, raised when the vehicle is 'swimming' water obstacles. (2) 9M14M Malyutka anti-tank missile. (3) Driver's hatch. (4) Gun elevation wheel assembly. (5) 1PN22M1 gunner's sight. (6) Turret hatch. (7) TNPO-170 gunner's periscope. (8) 73 mm ammunition. (9) Rear compartment access hatch. (10) MK-4s periscope. (11) Hydrojet water propulsion system for 'swimming'. (12) 5D20 engine. (13) Pneumatic suspension element. (14) Gunner's seat. (15) Used shell collector. (16) Driver's seat. (17) Track tension mechanism.

August 1968 were called Operation 'Danube'. The Soviet Army formed a Danube High Command, and organised three Fronts to support the operation. The Central Front, commanded by Col. Gen. Magarov, covered the Czech border from East Germany through to the Polish Silesian Military District. The Carpathian Front under Col. Gen. Bisyarin covered the Czechoslovak frontier from the Polish Warsaw Military District into the Soviet Union; and the Southern Front covered the Hungarian-Czechoslovak border. The VDV was ordered to mobilise two of its air assault divisions, of which one, the 103rd Guards Air Assault Division, would be used in a *coup de main* directed against Prague, with the other division in reserve. These forces were put directly under the Danube High Command. In addition, elements of the Polish 6th

The pneumatic suspension permits the height of the vehicle to be compressed when 'palletised' for an air drop—an effect seen clearly in this photo of a BMD-1M.

Pomeranian Air Assault Division were assigned the task of seizing the airfield at Pardubice.

On the evening of 20 August 1968 an unscheduled Aeroflot An-24 light transport aircraft approached Ruzyme Airport on the north-east outskirts of Prague and asked permission to land. This was granted, and the aircraft landed at about 2030 hrs and taxied to the end of the runway, where it parked. A second aircraft arrived shortly before midnight from Lviv in the Ukraine, and disembarked Soviet officials in civilian dress who talked briefly with Czech airport and state security officials before departing shortly afterwards. At midnight, as the troops of the Central and Carpathian Fronts began crossing the Czechoslovak frontier, the control tower received telephone instructions to close down. The airport swarmed with Soviet 'civilians' who began to take up positions around the field.

At about 0200 hrs on the morning of 21 August two military An-12 aircraft, escorted by MiG-21s, approached and landed at the airport. The An-12s taxied up to the airport buildings and rapidly disembarked two companies of *desantniki*, totalling about 180 troops. This advance group took over the airport from the 'civilian' team. With the airport secure, the command An-24, which had been sitting at the end of the runway since the beginning of the operation, ordered the first of five squadrons of An-12s of the VTA to begin landing the remainder of the 103rd Guards Air Assault Division's battle group. The landings were controlled from the fully equipped An-24 rather than the tower. The An-12s contained a number of ASU-85s and armoured personnel carriers, which were used to form a special assault team to seize the presidential palace on Hradcany Hill in Prague. The remainder of the division was used to surround key government buildings, communications centres and other facilities. At about 0600 hrs, after the Czechoslovak radio station in Prague announced that the invasion had occurred, the division was ordered to break in and seize all communication facilities. This was quickly accomplished. Shortly afterwards the lead elements of the 6th Guards Motor Rifle Division, at the head of the Central Front, began entering Prague, followed by armoured units of the 35th Motor Rifle Division. These units reinforced the 103rd Air Assault, and were allotted the main responsibilities for occupying Prague. Meanwhile, the airfield at Hradec Kralove had been seized by a helicopter assault unit, possibly one of the new formations of the VDV.

Operation 'Danube' provides a textbook example of Soviet airborne operations. A special Spetsnaz team, in this case in civilian clothes, occupies key administrative locations. The airborne force follows to seize the key target rapidly, but because of its relatively small size is quickly linked up with mechanised forces to control the objective.

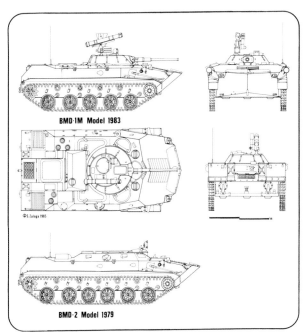

The BMD-1 Model 1973 has been the standard production version of this unique vehicle. It has the improved circular CBR air vent as compared with the square vent of the earlier Model 1970. This parading BMD is marked with the Guards insignia on the turret, and on the hull side with the badge shown as our Plate L2. (Sovfoto)

(Above) The re-engineered BMD-1M's most recognisable features are the new 'sunburst' pattern wheels replacing the earlier 'spoked' wheels; and the new grills in the upper hull front plate to improve ventilation. (Sovfoto)

(Below) A new variant of the BMD-1M was first displayed in 1983. The 9M14M Malyutka missile is replaced by the improved 9K111 Fagot, somewhat similar in size and performance to NATO's Milan anti-tank missile. (Sovfoto)

The VDV has been turning increasingly to the use of helicopters for the airlift rôle—in this case, an airmobile brigade operation during the 1984 'Shield' exercise in Czechoslovakia, using an Mi-8. (Sovfoto)

This operation ran relatively smoothly, if only because of the near total lack of Czech opposition.

The Invasion of Afghanistan

The invasion of Afghanistan in 1979 provides a slightly different picture of Soviet airborne envelopment techniques. The airborne forces allotted to the Afghan invasion were larger than those used in Czechoslovakia, probably due to the presumption that resistance was more likely. As in the case of Czechoslovakia, the VDV was to provide troops for a *coup de main* against the capital with the aim of eliminating the Afghan President, Hafizullah Amin, and installing in his place a new puppet government under Babrak Karmal.

A special VDV task force was formed under the command of Maj. Gen. Moussa Yevanov, consisting of one regiment each from the 103rd and 104th Guards Air Assault Divisions, and the entire 105th Guards Air Assault Division. In the first two weeks of December 1979 the Soviets began transferring about 1,500 additional personnel into Afghanistan, including a regiment of the 103rd Guards Air Assault Regiment on 7–9 December and a second regiment from the 104th on 21–22 December, to assist in controlling Bagram airport outside Kabul. Soviet advisers in Afghanistan began attempts to paralyse the Afghan armed forces by withdrawing armoured vehicles into motor pools for 'winterisation', and conducting 'inventories' on stocks of ammunition and missiles. Soviet advisers also

convinced Amin that the presidential palace on the outskirts of Kabul would be easier to defend against rebel attack than the residence in Kabul, and this helped to effectively isolate him from many loyal Afghan troops in the capital.

On 24 December 1979 the VDV forces at Bagram, 19 km outside Kabul, seized control of the airfield. This was quickly followed by the first of 280 sorties by VTA An-12s, An-22s and Il-76s, ferrying in the main elements of the 105th Guards Air Assault Division from its home base in Fergana in the neighbouring Turkestan Military District. Unlike the 1968 operation, the airborne troops in 1979 were fully mechanised with BMDs due to the distance to the capital and the greater likelihood of fighting. The airport was secured in five hours. Other Soviet divisions began crossing the Afghan border on 25 December, focusing on Kabul. With their base fully secured, the airborne forces began moving towards Kabul on the evening of 27 December, after most key government and communications buildings had been seized by Spetsnaz teams.

A special battle group, commanded by the former head of a KGB special operations school, Col. Bayerenov, was assembled to depose Amin at the Darulaman Palace. The interval between the initial landings at the Bagram air base and the actual move against the palace permitted Amin to gather a weak force of loyal troops around the palace, including a small number of tanks. The airborne task force, apparently using only lightly armoured BMDs and ASU-85s, assaulted the palace, losing several vehicles to the fire of the Afghan tanks. However, Afghan resistance was soon overcome, and Amin, his family, and his closest advisers were killed, probably by Soviet security personnel accompanying the task force.

The airborne units were later used to seize other key Afghan centres such as Kandahar, as well as the strategic Salang Pass. The main force remained in the Bagram air base area once the remainder of Soviet forces had entered Afghanistan throughout January 1980. Later in 1980 the airborne forces in Afghanistan were reorganised: the 105th Guards Airborne Division was disbanded and its place at Bagram was taken by the 103rd Guards Airborne Division. This unit is used as a reserve by Soviet forces in Afghanistan, and has been deployed on

Troops of the 36th Guards Naval Infantry Regt. receive political instruction during field exercises in the 1970s. Since this photo was taken the beret insignia have changed—see Plate D. (Sovfoto)

special operations. The 345th Guards Independent Air Assault Regiment is also apparently stationed at Bagram. There is also an air assault brigade, operating out of Shir Khan, which has seen extensive combat against the Islamic guerrillas.

The first VDV paratrooper to be decorated for conspicuous gallantry in action was Sr. Sgt. A. Mironenko, named in 1980 as a Hero of the Soviet Union, the highest Soviet military decoration. However, the Soviet press has generally played down the fighting in Afghanistan, and it was not until 1984 that any significant attention was paid to the efforts of the VDV. One of the few heroes to have emerged from the Afghanistan fighting was a young paratrooper, Sgt. Nikolai Chepik, who was assigned to a sapper unit, probably of the 103rd Air Assault Division. In February 1984 his squad was attacked by the *mujahadeen*, and Chepik was wounded twice in the legs. His squad was cornered, and as the *mujahadeen* closed in Chepik set off a stack of demolition charges or grenades, killing himself and

The principal armoured vehicle of the Naval Infantry is the BTR-60PB; these have only limited amphibious capability, and are as often as not landed on or very close to the beach from their *Polnocny* LSTs. (Sovfoto)

about 30 Afghans. He was posthumously named a Hero of the Soviet Union, and his exploits have been celebrated in the Soviet press ever since. Seven VDV troops have received this decoration up to the beginning of 1985.

Besides the combat deployments of airborne units in Afghanistan and Czechoslovakia, the VDV has been involved in a number of other operations. In the 1977 Ogaden desert war the VDV provided equipment and command personnel to the Ethiopian and Cuban forces, including BMDs which were airlifted behind Somali lines. In the 1973 crisis precipitated by the Yom Kippur War, the Soviet Army mobilised three airborne divisions as part of their threat of intervention in the Middle East fighting: reportedly, a regiment of the 106th Guards Air Assault Division was moved to Belgrade airport in anticipation of deployment to Syria.

The VDV Today

The VDV, under the command of Army Gen. D. Sukhorukov, currently fields seven air assault divisions, of which one, the 106th Guards Air Assault Division in the Tula-Ryazan area, is usually earmarked for training purposes. It would also appear that the 44th Guards Airborne Division at Jonava in the Baltic Military District is kept as a skeleton formation for training purposes, but is not war-ready, as the other seven divisions are. The current divisions and their stations are shown in the accompanying chart, although it should be borne in mind that there are certain discrepancies in the unclassified listings of these units.

These units are under the direction of the Ministry of Defence, and in time of war would serve as the primary strategic reserve of the STAVKA (High Command). Besides these units, the VDV appears to be responsible for the airmobile brigades and the air assault brigades. However, in contrast to the airborne divisions, these brigades are subordinate to the Ground Forces in their respective military districts. There are currently believed to be four airmobile brigades, ten air assault brigades, and an airmobile battalion with each forward-deployed tank or combined-arms Army.

The airborne divisions are based around three airborne regiments with supporting arms. This

Each Naval Infantry Regt. is supported by a tank battalion equipped with a mix of PT-76B amphibious and T-55 medium tanks. Here tank crews and infantrymen receive instruction prior to an operation. (Sovfoto)

The elderly PT-76B's amphibious capability makes it the principal tank of the Naval Infantry forces. The *Polnocny* class LST, seen here, represents the bulk of the Soviet landing ship fleet; it is in fact of Polish construction, being built at Gdansk—the Polish designation is ODS. (Sovfoto)

organisational structure is relatively loose in order to permit the divisions to be deployed in sub-divisional formations. A typical example would be an airborne regiment combat group with attached support units from elsewhere in the division, such as artillery and engineer support. Like the airborne division, the airborne regiment is triadic: its core is formed by three airborne battalions with support provided by an anti-aircraft battery, mortar battery, anti-tank battery, and other units. A more detailed picture is provided in the accompanying charts.

With a strength of about 6,500 troops, Soviet airborne divisions have considerably less manpower than units such as the US Army's 82nd Airborne Division, but have considerably more firepower

and mobility due to their mechanisation with about 320 BMDs. The Soviet and American airborne units are fundamentally different in orientation. Whereas the Soviet units are mechanised air assault units, the US units are light infantry air assault units.

The strategic mobility of the VDV's seven divisions is circumscribed by the airlift assets of the Soviet VTA (Military Transport Aviation). The VTA currently deploys about 600 medium and long range aircraft comprising 370 An-12, 170 Il-76 and 50 An-22. The An-12 has a range of 1,400 km, and can carry one or two BMDs; a single BMD-equipped airborne regiment requires 90 to 115 An-12 aircraft for an operation. The An-12 is being slowly replaced by the much-improved Il-76, which has a range of 5,300 km and can carry three BMDs or 120 *desantniki*. A BMD-equipped airborne regiment would require 50 to 65 Il-76 for a mission. The Il-76 and An-12 are supplemented by the

The mammoth AIST hovercraft are currently being adopted by the Soviet Navy in larger numbers; they are capable of carrying tanks, as evident in this view of a disembarking T-74. The Soviet Naval Infantry pioneered the use of hovercraft in amphibious landings. (Sovfoto)

enormous An-22 Antei, which can carry 175 troops or four BMDs to a maximum range of 4,200 km. Besides these assets, in wartime the VTA would probably absorb the 200 An-12 and Il-76 in Aeroflot service, although these are not configured for military cargoes.

Even with these additional aircraft, the VTA is capable of carrying only about one fully equipped airborne division on any long range mission, but could airlift two or three more lightly equipped divisions on shorter missions in a single surge. However, it is not at all clear that the entire resources of the VTA could be committed to a single operation due to its other responsibilities. On numerous occasions the VDV has demonstrated its ability to drop a considerable force with a single surge operation. For example, during the 1970 'Dvina' exercise, the 76th Guards Chenigov Air Assault Division, totalling about 8,000 troops and 160 vehicles, was dropped in 22 minutes. The gradual shift of the VDV from an airborne infantry force to an airborne mechanised force has greatly increased the airlift requirements of the divisions. A recent assessment of the airlift requirements for a single division, appearing in *Jane's Defence Weekly*, concluded that 639 Il-76 sorties would be required,

A T-55 of the Naval Infantry; normally each regiment has ten in its tank battalion, of which three are often the TO-55 flamethrower version. (Sovfoto)

Naval Infantry disembark from an AIST hovercraft. The main attraction of these craft is their ability to land their complement on shore and return quickly to the larger transports for another load. (Sovfoto)

A Naval Infantry platoon on exercises in 1983, supported by a BTR-60. These troops wear the normal black winter field uniform—cf. our Plate E2. (Sovfoto)

of which only six per cent would be devoted to manpower, 17 per cent to the BMDs, eight per cent to other armoured vehicles, guns and artillery, and 69 per cent to motor vehicles. Needless to say, this assessment makes it quite clear why the air assault divisions might be used without much of their heavy equipment for certain operations.

In spite of the limited airlift capability available to the VDV, its utility in Soviet strategic planning is quite considerable. The Soviets, like the Americans, appreciate that regional conflicts are far more likely to occur than any full-scale confrontation in Central Europe. The VDV is ideally suited for any regional requirement, being very heavily armed, well-trained and motivated, and well suited to rapid deployment by aircraft or other means. Significantly, the VDV has figured prominently in the two major Soviet military operations of the past two decades—Czechoslovakia and Afghanistan.

In the event of all-out war in Central Europe, the VDV could be employed in a variety of fashions. In an operational or strategic rôle, it could be used to seize key targets in NATO rear areas and to hold on to them until relieved by mechanised units. It is also

configured for exploiting tactical nuclear strikes in a conflict involving thermonuclear weapons. There are probably special KGB teams attached to these divisions for the use of atomic demolition munitions. On a tactical level, regimental or battalion-sized formations could be dropped or airlifted into the rear of NATO forces to strike at key communication or supply links, to threaten the rear of engaged NATO combat formations, to cut off retreating NATO units, and to wreak havoc in a variety of ways. At lower levels the VDV divisions are configured as combined-arms teams to permit their deployment in small battle groups. The presence of BMDs and Strela II anti-aircraft missiles at battalion level provides even these small formations with heavy firepower, anti-tank protection, high mobility and a modest air defence capability.

The air assault brigades are akin to a miniature airborne division, being somewhat less than half the size with about 2,000–2,600 troops. They consist of four air assault battalions, two of which are equipped with the BMD. Although paratroop qualified, their primary means of delivery would be by helicopters; as there are no organic helicopters in these formations, they would require the use of helicopters from neighbouring VVS Frontal Aviation units. A brigade with BMDs would require about 40 Mi-8 and 125 Mi-6 or Mi-26 sorties, while a brigade without its armour would require 75 Mi-8 and 35 Mi-6/Mi-26 sorties. The airmobile brigade is akin to the air assault brigade, but is much lighter in mechanised equipment and smaller in size, with only 1,700 to 1,900 troops. It has no BMDs and its only armour is 13 BRDMs, nine of which are the missile-firing anti-tank types. However, some sources claim that the airmobile brigades do have their own helicopters in the form of a composite regiment of 32 Mi-8 and 12 Mi-6/Mi-26. These are not adequate to lift the entire brigade in a single throw, but could lift about half the brigade without additional helicopters. Other sources maintain that the brigades have no organic helicopter support, and would have to rely on local air force units.

The combat utility of the VDV units is considerably enhanced by the selection and training of their troops. The VDV is allotted preferential selection of personnel, even before such favoured services as the nuclear submarine fleet and strategic rocket force. The main source of recruitment for the VDV is from DOSAAF-sponsored parachute clubs. The DOSAAF is a paramilitary agency which sponsors youth activities and paramilitary training. All Soviet students are obliged to participate in about 140 hours of pre-induction paramilitary training. Parachuting is a popular sport in the Soviet Union, actively encouraged by the government through DOSAAF. Much of the civilian equipment is essentially similar to the parachute gear used by the military, and the aircraft are mostly older VVS types like the ubiquitous An-2 biplane. Many *desantniki* can be

The new *Ivan Rogov* class of dock landing ships mark an important advance in Naval Infantry capabilities. They can operate with helicopters, and their rear dock can handle the new air-cushion landing craft with ease. The rear view shows the closed doors of the helicopter hangar above those of the large rear docking well area. (DoD/Mitsuo Shibata)

seen to be still wearing DOSAAF parachute decorations on their uniforms.

Besides the physical and mental conditioning that this pre-induction training provides, DOSAAF also actively promotes political training. The troops of the VDV are far more politically active than in the rest of the Army, and about 85 per cent are members either of the party or of the Communist youth organisation, the Komsomol. Although figures are not available, the VDV troops are probably disproportionately Russian, Byelorussian and Ukrainian, giving an added factor of political reliability. Beyond basic training, draftees are apparently cycled through an airborne training division before assignment to their division.

Training involves a more rigorous course of physical conditioning than in the rest of the Soviet Army. Specialised training includes normal combat jump training as well as more advanced techniques such as high altitude, low opening (HALO) for at least a portion of the troops. Officers of the VDV attend a special academy, the Ryazan Higher Airborne Command School. The airborne divisions are, except for the training divisions, Category I units, meaning that they are kept near to full strength in men and equipment in peacetime. This is in complete contrast to Ground Forces units, the majority of which are kept at a lower state of readiness.

The VDV is likely to remain in the forefront of any Soviet efforts to project military power beyond the borders of the USSR. For this reason, continued modernisation of these forces is likely. The Chief of Staff of the VDV, Lt. Gen. P. Pavlenko, hinted at this in an interview several years ago which appeared in a Soviet military journal: 'Military

thinking is focused on the future. Please note that in our force's name, the Air Assault Force, the word "parachute" is missing. The future of airborne operations looks more impressive than the present.' The VDV appears to be moving in two important directions. On the strategic level, the gradual replacement of the An-12 with the far more capable Il-76, and the replacement of the An-22 with the An-400 Condor, will finally permit the VDV to deploy divisions at far greater ranges than is currently possible. On the tactical level, the VDV appears to be at the forefront of adapting the helicopter to traditional VDV rôles, which will probably lead to a gradual shift of the VDV from being a force relying primarily on paratroop operations, to a more flexible force using air-landing, parachute and heliborne techniques to carry out its operations.

The Soviet Naval Infantry

The Soviet Naval Infantry is a far smaller force than the VDV, but enjoys a far longer tradition, tracing its lineage back to the landing parties of the Imperial Fleet of Peter the Great. It reached its peak during the Second World War, totalling over 350,000 troops in 40 brigades, six independent regiments, and a number of smaller units. Five of these brigades were honoured with the Guards distinction. Soviet accounts of the war indicate that 114 landings were carried out by these troops, but most of these were small raids by platoon or company-sized teams. There were only four amphibious operations during the war which involved several thousand landing troops: two on the Kerch peninsula, one at Novorossiysk on the Black Sea, and one at Moon Sound in the Baltic. The main reason for the abnormally large size of the Naval Infantry in the Second World War was the inactivity of the Soviet Fleet. Desperately short of manpower, the Red Army drew on the Fleet for troops and improvised units throughout the war; Naval Infantry were mainly used as ordinary foot soldiers with no particular amphibious training. Indeed, there was no better indication of the true

Soviet attitude towards these forces than the decision in 1947 to completely disband them. What few naval infantry units remained were sub-ordinated to the Coastal Defence Force. Attitudes eventually changed, and in 1961 the Naval Infantry was resurrected; the Soviet Army came to recognise the utility of specialised marine forces for conducting amphibious landings, and each of the fleets was allotted such a unit. Essential to this new policy was the development of amphibious warfare ships, notably the new LSTs of the Alligator class.

The Naval Infantry is divided between the four fleets. Since 1961 the Black Sea, Northern, and Baltic Fleets have been allotted a Naval Infantry regiment, while the Pacific Fleet has deployed a brigade. Recent US Intelligence assessments indicate that these formations may be larger, with brigades deployed by three fleets, and a division with the Pacific fleet. The table below uses their traditional description:

Unit		Base
63rd Gds. Kirkenneskaya Naval Inf. Regt.	...	Pechenga (Northern Fleet)
36th Guards Naval Inf. Regt.	...	Baltysk (Baltic Fleet)
(?) Guards Naval Inf. Regt.	...	Sevastapol (Black Sea Fleet)
(?) Guards Naval Inf. Bde.	...	Vladivostok (Pacific Fleet)

Each Naval Infantry Regiment comprises three naval motor rifle battalions and a naval tank battalion. The motor rifle battalions each have about 33 BTR-60 amphibious armoured troop carriers, while the tank battalion has a mixed complement of 34 PT-76 amphibious tanks and ten T-55 or T-72 tanks. In battalions with the T-55 tank, three of the ten are often the TO-55 flame-thrower type. A Naval Infantry brigade has two tank battalions and five battalions of naval motor rifle troops, making it nearly double the size of the 2,500-man regiments.

The Naval Infantry troops, like most Marine forces, are of a higher calibre than normal motor rifle troops of the Soviet Ground Forces. They are better trained than their Ground Forces counter-parts, and an increasing percentage are parachute qualified and trained in helicopter landing operations. There are apparently specialised teams in these regiments trained to employ atomic demolition munitions (ADM). Soviet ADMs are believed to be available in several types, weighing 70–80 lbs each, with an explosive force of .1 to .5 kilotons. They would be used to attack major port or seaside facilities.

The Soviet Naval Infantry force is quite small. It is intended for use on a tactical level as a raiding force, and on an operational level as the spearhead of an amphibious landing force. Once a beachhead had been seized, further troop landings would be provided by Ground Forces units. For this reason, the Soviet Naval Infantry numbers only about 18,000 troops—compared to the US Marine Corps, which is more than ten times its size. Likewise, the Soviet Fleet's amphibious warfare ships are inferior in number and sophistication to those of the US Navy. The Soviet Naval Infantry also differ considerably from the US Marines in their approach to amphibious warfare. While the US Marines have relied on specially designed armoured, amphibious tracked vehicles (amtracs) for landing operations, the Naval Infantry has used the normal Ground Forces BTR-60, which has only marginal performance in the water. This is due in no small measure to the difference in the experiences of the two forces. The US Marines have had a tradition of preparing for hotly contested beach assaults, such as those of the Second World War in the Pacific. In contrast, Soviet wartime experience was mainly against targets without formidable beach defences. Current areas where the Naval Infantry might be used, such as the Danish or Norwegian coasts, are not heavily fortified.

In contrast, the Soviet Naval Infantry have been ahead of the US Marines in the adaption of hovercraft for beach landing operations. The Soviet fleet has deployed over 60 hovercraft in three classes, most notably 35 of the AIST class, which is capable of carrying four PT-76 tanks, two T-72 tanks, or 220 troops; and a fourth new class of hovercraft, the Uteroks, are just beginning to enter service. The US, on the other hand, is only just beginning to deploy the new LCAC class of hovercraft. Hovercraft have obvious attractions over armoured amphibious vehicles: against lightly defended beaches, they can quickly land an assault force, and return rapidly alongside the ships of the assault fleet to load up for renewed missions to the beachhead.

Judging by the Soviet Navy's current shipbuilding programmes, the future of the Soviet Naval Infantry seems assured, and its rôle in Soviet strategic thinking is likely to increase. In contrast to the situation in recent years, with the strategic employment of the Naval Infantry restricted both by its small size and by lack of modern amphibious landing ships, its recent growth, coupled with the construction of further *Ivan Rogov* class landing ships, makes it more suitable for employment outside traditional Soviet waters. The Naval Infantry is no longer confined to LSTs alone: the *Ivan Rogov* class has habitable berths on board for the Naval Infantry, thus permitting long voyages to more distant destinations. This point has been illustrated by Soviet landing exercises in Syria in recent years.

Experience in Afghanistan has prompted the Soviet Army to take greater interest in mountain infantry training. It is not yet clear whether the new mountain units, like this one, are specialist units with their own identity, or simply motor rifle troops with expanded training.

Other Soviet Specialised Troops

Specialised infantry

Although the Red Army of the Second World War had specially trained mountain infantry and mountain cavalry divisions, these units largely disappeared after the 1950s. In the 1980s, due to experience in Afghanistan, the Ground Forces have begun to reassess this move. Normal motor rifle units lack the experience to operate effectively in mountainous terrain, and lack certain specialised equipment (e.g. rappelling gear) for particularly severe terrain such as is often encountered in Central Asia and Afghanistan. As a result, in the early 1980s, the Soviets appear to have begun to provide specialised mountain warfare training to certain motor rifle regiments, although it is not clear whether these units are being converted to mountain infantry regiments, or merely being trained to operate under special mountain conditions. The Ground Forces also deploy units with specialised arctic training in the Leningrad Military District. These motor rifle divisions employ the MT-LBV in place of the BTR-60 or BMP, due to its better performance in snow, and receive extensive ski training.

SPETSNAZ

The Spetsnaz are the special operations troops directed by Soviet Military Intelligence, the GRU. In contrast to normal élite formations, Spetsnaz are intended to engage in less conventional, diversionary warfare. They are descendants of specially trained teams who were parachuted behind the lines during the Second World War to support and inflame partisan activity.

Contemporary Spetsnaz units are trained primarily for attacking high value targets such as nuclear weapons stockpiles, theatre nuclear forces, airfields and command and communication centres, as well as other diversionary tasks. The basic Spetsnaz unit is the Special Operations Brigade (*Brigada osobovo*

The KGB Border Guards are amply equipped with helicopters and armoured vehicles. These assets are usually contained in military district reserve units, used to support Border Guard Detachments for specific missions. The Mi-8 is the standard helicopter in this rôle, although Mi-24 Gorbach units are also deployed on the Chinese frontier. (Sovfoto)

naznacheniya) which consists of three or four airborne battalions. There are apparently 16 of these brigades, allotted one per group-of-forces or military district. Like the airmobile and air assault brigades, the special operations brigades would be commanded by the local army or front commanders in time of war. A proportion of Spetsnaz troops are also trained for more demanding tasks such as assassination, leading Communist insurgent groups, or carrying out rear area sabotage operations. Some Spetsnaz units are also trained to carry out operations disguised as foreign troops. The Spetsnaz are a counterpart of Allied Ranger, SAS or 'Green Beret' units, and are often called by the traditional Russian names for such troops: *razvedchiki* (scouts) or *vysotniki* (rangers). Reports indicate the presence of eight specially trained commando battalions based with Group of Soviet Forces–Germany at Neurippen. These are believed to be an enlarged Spetsnaz brigade which would be divided in the event of war to provide a brigade to each of the two Fronts formed by the Group of Soviet Forces–Germany.

The special operations brigades have a direct counterpart naval formation, the naval special operations brigades, which are allotted one to each of the four fleets. These are organised around three battalions of combat swimmers, an airborne battalion, a supporting midget submarine unit, and specialist troops. The naval special operations brigades are intended to support amphibious operations by beach clearing and scouting; and they can also be used for independent offensive operations such as harbour raids. Their closest NATO counterparts are the British SBS or the US Navy SEALS and UDT.

The Spetsnaz are earmarked for especially difficult assignments and are the *crème de la crème* of the élite units of the Soviet Armed Forces. Their existence is shrouded in secrecy, and as a result, they are not permitted any distinctive form of uniform or insignia. Their service dress is usually that of corresponding services, such as airborne forces or naval infantry, and their field dress would be much the same. Little is known of Spetsnaz operations, for obvious reasons. There have been numerous reports of the use of special commando teams in Afghanistan, which could be Spetsnaz operations. The activity of Soviet frogmen off the coast of

KGB Border Guards photographed in May 1980 wearing the new *kamuflirovanniy kurtki* uniform, of standard Soviet camouflage cloth but cut like a service dress and worn with all appropriate badges, collar tabs and shoulder boards: cf. Plate C3. (Photo courtesy William Fowler)

Sweden can probably be traced to the Spetsnaz, though reports that several have been killed by Swedish coastal defence forces have been vigorously denied by the Swedish government. There have been reports that the KGB has formed its own counterparts to the Spetsnaz for diversionary activity in wartime, but no details of such units are available.

Security Units

The Soviet Union supports two organisations to prevent anti-government actions: the KGB (Committee for State Security) and the MVD (Ministry of Internal Security). Both organisations have military units which are part of the Soviet Armed Forces, but which are not under Defence Ministry control. These units are not military élites in the Western sense, and indeed they lack direct Western counterparts. Rather, they are a form of political/military élite. Recruitment into these units serves in lieu of regular military service, and entrance into certain of the units is far more tightly controlled than into most military units. The security apparatus forms the third leg of the triad of Soviet state power, comparable to the Army and the Communist Party. It keeps its eye on the other two elements of the Soviet state, as well as on the

A Border Guard squad prepare for patrol; they make extensive use of dogs, and this Alsatian pup is probably being trained. (Sovfoto)

counterpart. The Border Guards have many of the same rôles as normal border security forces: they provide the personnel to man immigration check points, airport passport controls, train inspection teams, and border crossings. However, the Border Guards are also responsible for sealing the Soviet borders from both internal and external penetration. Their rôle is to prevent the unauthorised escape of Soviet citizens from the USSR, to prevent border smuggling, to suppress ethnic dissident movements in the frontier regions, and to repel any incursions by foreign military units until the arrival of other elements of the Soviet Army. For these purposes the Border Guards are equipped with tanks, armoured personnel carriers, small warships, armed helicopters, and light military aircraft.

The Border Guards have had a long tradition of combat action along the lengthy Soviet frontier. The two most persistent trouble spots have been the Central Asian frontier areas and the border with China. Since the 1920s the Soviet Union has had trouble with its Islamic peoples, and Islamic rebels and smugglers—called *basmachi* by the Russians—have been a thorn in the side of the Border Guards. There have been innumerable campaigns and engagements by the Border Guards in this region, the most current variation on the theme being the situation in Afghanistan. The Border Guards have provided troops to quell the *mujahadeen* along the border area with Afghanistan, and to combat the occasional incursion of rebel Afghan fighters into the USSR itself. (Among past Border Guards who have been involved in these campaigns was the young Konstantin Chernenko in the 1930s.)

The other trouble spot has been the eastern border region. In the 1920s and 1930s the USSR had continuing problems with the Chinese warlords and their claims to territory along the eastern borders. The most serious of these outbreaks was fought over control of the Far Eastern Railway spur of the Trans-Siberian Magistral Railway in the late 1920s, when Border Troops were provided with Army tank units. In the early 1930s the enemy in this region became the Japanese, and an undeclared war was fought along the border. The Border Guards bore the brunt of the early fighting, which finally culminated in full scale battles in 1938 and 1939. In the 1960s the Border Guards were heavily involved in fighting with the Chinese Army over the

citizenry in general. In return for loyalty to the security apparatus, members of these organisations are afforded privileges not found elsewhere in Soviet society, such as access to housing and consumer goods which are otherwise difficult to obtain. In some respects, the members of the security apparatus and their families form a caste separate from the rest of Soviet society. This separation is encouraged by the state, since excessive fraternisation with the rest of Soviet society might serve to undermine their commitment to uphold the state against any internal enemies.

The largest KGB military force are the **Border Guards**, numbering about 175,000 troops. While several European countries have border forces, none match the military complexion of their Soviet

disputed territories along the Chinese and Soviet borders such as Damanskiy Island. These encounters are often mistakenly thought to have been fought by regular Ground Forces troops, as the Border Guards' uniforms and equipment are identical to those of the Ground Forces, although the shoulder boards carry the Cyrillic letters 'PV' rather than the 'SA' of the Soviet Army.

The Border Guards are organised into nine military border districts, distinct from the military districts of the rest of the armed forces. These districts vary in depth, running from three to 600 kilometres from the frontier. On average, the districts form a restricted zone about 42 km deep. Within these districts there are individual Border Guard Detachments, usually responsible for a length of the frontier of 100 to 600 km. These detachments are roughly of battalion strength (about 500 troops) and are organised into an HQ, a manoeuvre group and a *komendatura*. The *komendatura* provides the basic outpost service, with five platoon-sized outpost units, a reserve outpost platoon, as well as an HQ and service unit. Each

line outpost platoon has three rifle squads, a heavy machine gun squad and a dog section, plus attached signal and support sections. The *komendatura* absorbs the bulk of the unit's troops. The manoeuvre group is a detachment reserve force to back up any of the outposts in the event of major problems, and usually consists of two rifle platoons, a light machine gun platoon and a heavy machine gun platoon.

Besides the basic Border Guard Detachment, there are a variety of other Border Guard units including helicopter patrol and mechanised units. Perhaps the most enigmatic of the Border Guard units are the Mi-24 Gorbach helicopter units stationed on the Chinese border. As a result of the fighting in the late 1960s, the KGB and Soviet Army co-operated in the development of an armed helicopter suitable for patrolling the long, contested Chinese frontier. The result was the famous Mi-24, which differs from NATO attack helicopters in that it can carry an eight-man squad in addition to its heavy armament. This was developed to make it suitable for carrying small Border Guard units to inspect or man trouble points along the frontier. The Mi-24 is now better known for its anti-tank rôle in VVS helicopter regiments and, of course, for its use in Afghanistan, than for the KGB requirement that spawned it.

In time of war, the Border Guards have traditionally served to form special security units, which have been used to suppress anti-Soviet partisan groups in the USSR and neighbouring states, to put down army mutinies, and occasionally to clean up pockets of enemy resistance left behind Soviet lines.

Border Guards are recruited on the basis of a competitive examination, and service in the force counts in lieu of normal Soviet Army service. Although details are lacking, the Border Guards make preferential selection from applicants of Russian, Byelorussian and Ukrainian nationality.

The Border Guards are the largest, but not the only, military units of the KGB. The KGB also has an élite Kremlin Guard unit, the descendant of the original *Vecheka* units of 1917, which guard the centre of Soviet government. These troops can be distinguished from the Border Guards by their arm-of-service colour, which is royal blue instead of green. The KGB also has special guards units for high state officials, and to protect certain especially

This US DoD sketch shows a Spetsnaz training facility, with full-scale mock-ups of NATO weapons including the GLCM cruise missile, Pershing II launcher, and other high-value targets on which Spetsnaz would be tasked in wartime. (DoD)

sensitive installations, notably nuclear weapons stockpiles. Few details are known. Their shoulder boards are marked with the letters 'GB' instead of the 'PV' of the Border Guards.

The MVD (the Ministry of Internal Security) has its own troops which are known as the **Interior Army** (*Vnutrennie Voiska*)—a larger counterpart to the Border Guards, and as its name implies, responsible for combating anti-state activity inside the USSR. It numbers about 260,000 troops, formed into conventional military units with their own artillery and armour, and equivalent to about 30 motor rifle divisions. The majority of the draftees are trained as conventional motor rifle troops, but by MVD schools and not the Ground Forces. The MVD seems to favour induction of politically unsophisticated recruits from backward rural regions, especially Central Asia, who prove more amenable to indoctrination, show greater appreciation for the modest privileges afforded them, and prove more reliable in carrying out their duties. The Interior Army prefers Central Asian, Russian and East Ukrainian recruits and generally excludes Jews and Balts. When asked why the Interior Army favours Central Asians, a former Soviet Army officer responded: 'Because they are known for their obedience, stupidity and cruelty. They do everything they are asked without thinking, and are especially mean towards Russians.'

The rôle of the Interior Army is quite varied. It provides troops to guard a wide variety of installations, including certain major food storage areas (due to the perennial Soviet problem of pilfering). Probably its most concentrated use is in its guard services for the 1,100 labour camps (*Gulag*) still in operation in the USSR; these require the services of the equivalent of five divisions of Interior Army troops. The Interior Army also serves as a counterbalance to the Soviet Army in the event of army mutinies; on major Soviet Army bases, the ammunition stockpiles are under Interior Army control. Other Interior Army units are distributed throughout the country, and form a stiff reinforcement for local militia units if strikes or demonstrations get out of hand. The largest of these units is the Dzerzhinskiy Special Operations Motor Rifle Division in Moscow. In most cities, the units are smaller than divisional strength, often consisting of an infantry battalion or less, and backed up by a small number of light tanks and other light armour.

Although it may seem superfluous to maintain such a large force as a counterweight to popular unrest in view of the availability of the enormous Soviet Army, several factors argue against using the Soviet Army in this rôle. To begin with, many units of the Ground Forces do not have the political reliability for such duties since the troops are apt to be sympathetic to certain popular outbursts. Furthermore, the Army has traditionally found such service to be distasteful. The Soviet Army is genuinely popular amongst many elements of Soviet society, and the cultivation of this popularity is not helped by engagement in internal security work. While this sensitivity may seem odd in the army of a totalitarian state, the Soviet Army realises that any popular resentment aroused by its use on internal security duties would probably undermine its efforts to maintain military discipline, and would hamper attempts to persuade draftees to make a career in the armed forces. It is far easier to work in an environment where the Army is accepted and even admired, than in a situation where it is deeply resented.

During wartime the Interior Army continues to be responsible for its regular functions, and has additional war rôles. In the past, 'blocking units' (*zagraditelnye otriady*) have been formed to prevent Soviet Army units or stragglers from fleeing the front lines. The Interior Army has also traditionally been responsible for forming 'hunter units' (*istrebitelnye otriady*) which are used to suppress internal, anti-Soviet partisan groups among dissaffected minorities, as well as to root out any enemy forces left behind Soviet lines. In these circumstances, these units tend to fall under KGB control.

Elite Forces of the Warsaw Pact

Poland

The Polish People's Army (*Ludowe Wojsko Polskie*) is the largest of the Soviet's Warsaw Pact allies, and has the only other divisional-sized élite formations—an airborne division and a marine division. Poland also has a variety of internal security units which closely parallel Soviet models. The Polish armed forces present an interesting example of the organisational tensions which are created by the attempts of a Communist state to develop reliable, well-motivated military units to support Soviet military aims in the midst of a society that is profoundly anti-Russian.

The Polish Army has a modest but proud tradition of airborne units. Prior to the Second World War there was some experimentation with army paratroops, culminating in the formation of a Military Parachute Centre at Bydgoszcz in 1938. Following the defeat of Poland in 1939, the army-in-exile formed in Britain began in the summer of 1940 the creation of paratroop units which would eventually emerge as the 1st Polish Independent Paratroop Brigade. This unit eventually saw combat in the ill-fated Arnhem operation. In the east, the Communist-led Polish People's Army formed by the Red Army created an independent Polish Assault Battalion; this was not deployed as a complete unit, but elements of it were dropped behind German lines in support of the AL—the Communist Polish partisan movement. Following the war the LWP apparently maintained a small paratroop force, but details are lacking.

In 1957 the 6th Pomeranian Infantry Division was reorganised as an airborne division along Soviet lines, and designated the *6 Pomorska Dywizja Powietrzna-Desantowa* (6 PDPD)—6th Pomeranian Air Assault Division. It is stationed outside Krakow in the Warsaw Military District, and differs considerably from Soviet airborne divisions. It is smaller, with a strength of only about 4,000 troops, and is not heavily mechanised, lacking the BMD of the Soviet units. It uses the OT-64 SKOT and the BMP in lieu of the BMD, but how these vehicles are integrated into the division is not clear. In this respect it is probably somewhat closer in organisation to the Soviet airborne divisions of the 1970s, with a single mechanised regiment, than to the current Soviet configuration. The only special

Men of the Polish 6th Pomeranian Air Assault Div. explain their equipment to a visitor during a public display in the 1960s. The old-style 'splinter' camouflage clothing, and the antiquated PPSh, have both given way to new equipment since this photo was taken: cf. Plate F.

armoured airborne equipment used by the division was the ASU-85, which was unpopular in Polish service and was retired several years ago. Details on the organisation of the division are not known but it is believed to be based around four airborne battalions, and a special operations battalion.

The 6th Pomeranian Air Assault Division is an élite formation like its Soviet counterparts, and can draw on Polish sky-diving clubs to support recruitment. Jump training includes 15 'combat' jumps per year, not counting training jumps, for all its troops including even cooks and bandsmen. The division also specialises in mountain and arctic warfare, and practises in the nearby Carpathian mountains south of its Krakow base. The division has long enjoyed a maverick reputation in Poland, which probably helps recruitment. There have been long-standing rumours that the divisional command was reorganised after 1968 due to its reluctance to become involved in suppressing

student strikes in Krakow in 1967–68, or to participate in the 1968 invasion of Czechoslovakia. (Elements of the division were still used to seize Czechoslovakia's Pardubice air base, however.) The paratroops have a reputation for occasional brawls with state security units. Since the martial law crackdown, the division, under the command of Gen. Marian Zdrzalka, has been given the nickname of 'Jaruzelski's Circus'. This name stems from the assumption that the division, which is loyal to the Army hierarchy, would be used as a counterbalance in any internal Polish dispute involving attempts by the 'concrete' faction of the Polish Communist Party and the security apparatus to mount a coup against Jaruzelski.

The rumours and myths surrounding the division highlight the difficulty of raising reliable élite units to support Soviet military objectives in wartime when the surrounding society is so intensely anti-Soviet. The Polish technique has generally been to accent the national tradition of the military, which is quite effective, due to the genuine and traditional popularity of the Polish Army among civilians. The

The 6 PDPD on exercise in the 1960s; note the old-style cloth jump helmet, and the battalion (?) insignia on the officer's shoulder.

Soviet VDV:
1: Paratrooper, summer jump uniform, 1980s
2: Paratrooper, winter jump uniform, 1980s
3: Sleeve patch, Air Assault Div.
4: Sleeve patch, Air Assault Bde. (provisional)

A

1: Paratrooper, VDV, summer combat dress, 1980s
2: 'Spetsnaz', KGB Border Guards uniform, Afghanistan
3: Soviet Mountain Infantry, Afghanistan

B

1: Officer, VDV armoured unit, early 1980s
2: Paratrooper, VDV, field service dress, early 1980s
3: KGB Border Guard, field service dress, early 1980s

C

1: Soviet Naval Infantry, combat dress, 1975
2: Soviet Naval Infantry, combat dress, 1985
3: Soviet Naval Infantry sleeve patch

D

1: Captain 2nd Rank, Soviet Naval Inf., summer
   field service dress, 1985
2: Soviet Naval Inf., winter field dress, 1985
3: Soviet Naval Inf. tank crew commander, 1985

E

Polish 6 Pomeranian Air Assault Division:
1: Paratrooper, jump uniform, 1970
2: Officer, summer field service dress, 1985
3: Paratrooper, winter combat dress, 1985
4: Current divisional patch
5: Unidentified unit patch, 1970s

F

3: Polish Podhale WOP Mountain Bde.; service dress, 1985

4: 7th Naval Assault Div. patch

5: Podhale WOP Mountain Bde. patch

2

3

1

1: WO, Polish 7th Naval Assault Div.; summer field service dress, 1970s-80s
2: Polish Naval Assault Infantry, winter combat dress, 1985

G

1: Officer, Czechoslovak 22nd Abn. Regt.; field
   service dress, 1980
2: Paratrooper, 22nd Abn.Regt.; summer combat
   dress, 1985

3: Czechoslovak 22nd Abn.Regt. sleeve patch
4: Czechoslovak airborne arm-of-service insignia
5: Vehicle marking, 22nd Abn.Regt.

H

1: Unterfeldwebel, NVA 40th Abn.Bn.; walking-out
   dress, 1985
2,3: Paratroopers, NVA 40th Abn.Bn.; summer combat
   dress, 1985

I

1: Bulgarian Paratrooper, combat dress, 1980s
2,3: Bulgarian Mountain Infantry, summer field dress, 1985

J

1: Paratrooper, Romanian 161st Para Regt.; summer jump uniform, 1980s

2: Romanian Mountain Infantry, summer field service dress, 1980s

3: Bulgarian airborne arm-of-service insignia

4: Vehicle marking, Romanian 161st Para Regt.

5: Romanian mountain troops arm-of-service insignia

K

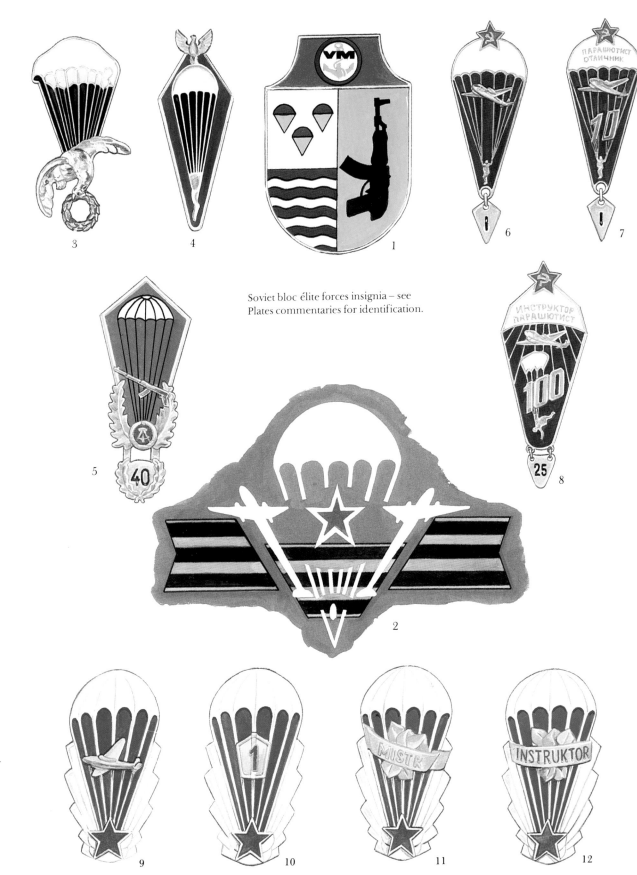

3   4   1   6   7

Soviet bloc élite forces insignia – see
Plates commentaries for identification.

5   8   2

9   10   11   12

L

Army attempts to deflect any anti-Soviet hostility by playing up the 'revanchist' territorial claims on western Poland by certain extremist West German parties. Besides stirring up anti-German sentiment, the Army also tries to accent any rôles in which Polish forces may be used that are particularly relevant to Polish interests. For example, in the 6th Pomeranian Air Assault Division considerable attention is paid to the use of the division in attacking and destroying US or West German theatre missiles like the Pershing and cruise missile, which could be targeted on Soviet logistics links running through Poland. Some pride is also taken in attempts to better the performance of Soviet units in joint Warsaw Pact manoeuvres. The Poles, Czechs, Slovaks and Germans tend to be rather contemptuous of their Soviet counterparts, due to what they see as their higher level of military professionalism. The actual issue of the reliability of units like this in the event of a war in Central Europe is very hard to assess, given the many conflicting factors which affect unit effectiveness, morale and cohesion. It should not be forgotten that

The 6 PDPD uses the WP-8 rocket launcher for fire support, seen here towed behind a UAZ-469 jeep during a parade. The crew wear the standard Polish paratrooper helmet. (Eastfoto)

although the troops of the Polish LWP in 1943–45 were no less anti-Soviet than their current counterparts, they loyally fought alongside the Soviet Army. Yet neither can it be taken for granted that units like this will prove reliable in the event of another major European war. It is not clear whether the military professionalism of such units would overcome the traditional antipathy of their society to fight effectively on the Soviet side.

Recent articles in the Polish military press

Polish paras on mountain training in the Carpathians, man-handling a B-10 82 mm recoilless rifle.

Though much more lightly mechanised than comparable Soviet formations, the Polish 6 PDPD has a modest number of OT-64 SKOT armoured personnel carriers.

indicate that the 6th Pomeranian Air Assault Division is the subject of some discussion regarding future rôles and organisation. Like the Soviet airborne divisions, it would appear that the 6 PDPD will be gradually shifting towards greater reliance on helicopters for tactical mobility. This is a sound move in the Polish case, since the division has a minimal strategic rôle and little need for extreme long range capability.

The 6PDPD has an independent special operations battalion, formerly designated the 4101st Paratroop Battalion. This unit is reportedly trained in rear area scouting and sabotage, and is under the direction of the WSW counter-intelligence force rather than the normal Army chain of command. During the 1985 trial of four security police officers for the murder of pro-Solidarity activist Father Jerzy Popieluszko, the military provided troops from an 'anti-terrorist' unit to supplement the state militia. These troops wore a variation of the 6 PDPD insignia but on a green rather than a red background, and wore black rather than red berets. These may have been troops of this highly secret unit. The Poles also deploy a special guard unit to protect high government officials, called BOR (*Batalion Ochrony Rządu*).

Somewhat more enigmatic than the 6th Pomeranian Air Assault Division is its counterpart marine formation. This is euphemistically referred to as the JOW (*Jednostka Obrona Wybrzeza*: Coastal Defence Unit) in public sources, which implies a small collection of defensive units comparable to the pre-war *Ladowa Obrona Wybrzeza* which commanded army and naval infantry units in the 1939 defence of the Polish coast. In fact, this unit was formed by reorganising the 23rd Mechanized Division and 3rd Marine Regiment into a marine assault division, and is believed to be designated 7 *Luzycka Dywizya Desantnowa-Morska* (7 LDDM)— the 7th Luzycka Naval Assault Division. Based at Gdansk, it is a regular Army unit and not under Navy jurisdiction. Although a division by Warsaw Pact standards, it is only about a third of the size of a US Marine Division, with about 5,500 troops. It is organised into three assault regiments each with five companies of OT-62 TOPAS-borne marines and a company of 13 PT-76 amphibious tanks. There are a total of about 60 TOPAS per regiment, of which ten carry 82 mm mortars. The division has an organic 'Frog' rocket, anti-aircraft, BM-21 Grad-P Katyusha, tank and recce battalion, as well as associated service and support units. The 7th Naval Assault Division is intended to support the amphibious operations of the Soviet Baltic Fleet in conjunction with the 36th Guards Naval Infantry Regiment and the Polish Navy. Although the division could be used for raiding operations, its strategic rôle is believed to be the invasion of Denmark alongside Soviet and German units.

Besides the 7th Naval Assault Division, the Polish Navy is believed to have a modest naval infantry force of about two battalions, mainly intended for defensive purposes. The Navy also has a number of naval combat swimmer units trained in underwater

Fire support for the Polish 7th Luzycka Naval Assault Div. is provided by the standard Warsaw Pact BM-21 Grad-P 122 mm multiple rocket launcher.

demolitions of both an offensive and defensive character.

The Poles have a bewildering variety of internal security forces ranging from police militias up to military security brigades with attached armoured units. The rationale for these units is not particularly difficult to understand. Poland has been a hotbed of anti-Soviet and anti-state trouble since 1945. The Polish Army has generally tried to distance itself from the internal security rôle, since this tends to undermine its popularity in Polish society and complicates the already difficult task of recruiting and holding on to talented personnel— internal security operations tend to undermine unit morale. In the 1945–49 period there was a bloody civil war between remnants of the non-Communist underground (both Polish and Ukrainian) and Communist security forces. Although the Army was used during these anti-partisan operations, especially against the Ukrainian UPA, it did not prove particularly reliable in dealing with Polish underground forces. This led to the formation of special military units of the Ministry of Internal Affairs, the KBW.

In 1956, when the Army refused to fire on striking workers in Poznan, a KBW brigade was brought in; this resulted in the expected level of bloodshed. In October 1956 the KBW, including its armoured units, was used to support the coup by Gomulka to seize power and to threaten the Soviets to refrain from intervening in the Polish political crisis. The KBW garnered a well-deserved reputation for brutality in dealing with anti-government protests, and in 1965 was put under Ministry of National Defence control and reorganised as the WOW (*Wojska Obrony Wewnetrznej:* Internal Defence Army). The WOW is under the command of the Territorial Defence Forces (OTK), and is a direct counterpart of the Soviet Interior Army (VV). The WOW is currently organised into regiments, of which there are believed to be 17, one per province. They are named after the region in which they are stationed; for example, the *Pulk WOW Kaszubski* is the WOW Regiment in the Kaszub region. Like the Soviet Interior Army, they

The 7 LDDM's principal armoured vehicle is the OT-62 TOPAS, a derivative of the Soviet BTR-50 which is manufactured jointly by Poland and Czechoslovakia. This is the standard Polish version, the TOPAS 2AP, with the new turret. Just visible on the hull side above the rear hydrojet vent is the divisional insignia—see Plate G.

appear to be trained as motorised infantry troops. They wear Polish Army uniforms with distinctive arm-of-service insignia, but in some cases use different equipment (e.g. some units use the BTR-60 in place of the OT-64).

The other element of the Polish military security apparatus used to back up the state police (militia) is the WSW (*Wojskowa Sluzba Wewnetrzna:* Army Internal Service). Although nominally a military police unit, the WSW is under the control of military counter-intelligence and numbers about 25,000 troops. Whereas WOW has been used to back up the militia in dealing with popular discontent, the WSW appears to be tasked with suppressing trouble in the armed forces. There is ample reason for anxiety in this area, as many army units have refused to become involved in suppressing strikes and demonstrations. Nevertheless, use of the WOW and WSW is usually a matter of last resort, as was the case in the early 1980s when the many confrontations with the Solidarity movement led to the imposition of martial law. The civilian security apparatus has a much larger organisation

A single brigade of the Polish Frontier Guards (WOP) maintain the Polish mountain infantry tradition, wearing this unique uniform derived from the folk costume of the Podhale (highland) region. There are few changes from the uniform worn by mountain infantry up to 1939. The Podhalanska Brygada WOP is a favourite at ceremonial public parades. (Eastfoto)

for dealing with popular discontent: the Ministry of Internal Affairs directs the SB (the Polish equivalent of the KGB) while its strong-arm requirements are satisfied by the Militia (MO) and the brutal para-military wing of the police, the ZOMO.

Apart from the WOW, the OTK also directs the WOP (*Wojska Ochrony Pogranicza:* Border Defence Force), which is a direct Polish equivalent of the Soviet Border Guards or the pre-war Polish KOP. The WOP serves most of the same functions as the Soviet Border Guards, in terms of immigration and passport control, border checks and border patrols. Since Poland lacks any serious border problems apart from the occasional escaping citizen and a certain amount of smuggling, a significant portion of the WOP is allotted to military duties. The WOP is organised into brigades, which are named after the border districts in which they are stationed. Most of the units wear normal Polish Army uniforms, with the characteristic green arm-of-service insignia of the WOP. However, the *Brygada WOP Podhalanska* (WOP Highland Brigade) carries on the Polish mountain infantry tradition and is outfitted in a uniform derived from that of the pre-war mountain infantry regiments. It is an élite unit in the WOP, and is put through strenuous training in the rugged Carpathian mountains of southern Poland. In wartime, the WOP and WOW would be used to provide rear area security. The WOW is specially trained to deal with long range enemy recce units.

East Germany

The East German NVA (*Nationale Volksarmee:* National People's Army) deploys one airborne battalion, a naval landing-qualified regiment, and a number of specialised diversionary units. It is considered by many observers to be the most professional of the Warsaw Pact forces, though it is smaller than the Polish or Czechoslovak armies. It is also the most tightly controlled, with extensive contacts with Soviet command elements.

The airborne unit is the 40. ('Willi Sanger') Fallschirmjäger Bataillon stationed at Proro on Rugen Island in the Baltic. There are frequently cited references to two other battalions, the 2nd and the 5th, but these are both earlier designations of the 40th Airborne Battalion. The 40th Airborne Battalion was added to the NVA order-of-battle

In the field, paratroopers of the East German NVA's 40th Battalion wear this plain grey-brown beret, for concealment: cf. Plate I.

only in 1973, by expanding an airborne company at Cottbus. The battalion is under the direct command of the Ministry of Defence, separate from the Military District commands; and like the Soviet airborne divisions, it forms a high command reserve in time of war. The battalion appears to be very lightly equipped compared to other Warsaw Pact airborne units, with apparently little or no armour, and only a modest amount of motorised equipment. They are frequently referred to as 'commando' troops in the German press, and are intended for rear area raiding activities.

At least one NVA motor rifle regiment, the 29th 'Ernst Moritz Arndt' Regiment, has trained with the Soviet 36th Guards Naval Infantry Regiment for amphibious operations in the Baltic. It is based at Proro on Rugen Island in the northern DDR and is attached to the 8th Motor Rifle Division of the Northern Army (Military District). The unit appears to be structured like normal motor rifle regiments, but additional training has presumably been provided to familiarise its troops with the landing ships and landing craft which would be

East German paras on exercise; the second soldier carries the special airborne troops' version of the RPG-7 anti-tank rocket launcher, the 'knock-down' RPG-7D. This is currently being replaced in Soviet units by the RPG-16D.

used in the event of amphibious operations. Its vehicles occasionally display a white anchor emblem.

Besides these units, the Ministry of Defence has available a number of smaller élite groups. In southern Germany there is a special diversionary battalion equipped with M113s and M48s which were obtained from Vietnam. These armoured vehicles are painted in West German markings, and the unit's troops are equipped and dressed like a regular West German mechanised unit. They would be used in time of war for unconventional operations to penetrate NATO lines and may be subordinate to the MfS instead of the Ministry of Defence. The Volksmarine (Navy) has a number of *Kampfschwimmer* (combat swimmer) companies, which are paratroop-qualified and are intended to support amphibious operations or for raiding. They are trained in explosives disposal as well as in combat demolitions.

The East Germans deploy proportionately one of the largest internal security forces within the Warsaw Pact. The most significant of these are the *Grenztruppen der DDR*, the East German Frontier Troops, numbering about 50,000 men. These are the direct equivalent of the Soviet Border Guards. Although the original German Frontier Police had been under the control of the Minister of the Interior, in 1961 these forces were transferred to the Minister of Defence and reorganised along military lines. The headquarters of the Frontier Troops is in Paetz, and they are currently controlled by the Deputy Defence Minister, Maj. Gen. Klaus-Dieter Baumgarten.

The Frontier Troops are divided into three main military zones, plus the coast. The Coastal Frontier Command operating from Rostock controls one brigade of twelve independent battalions and two boat battalions, and is under Navy control. The Frontier Command North, headquartered in Stendal, deploys six Frontier Troop regiments, a helicopter flight and two training regiments. Frontier Command South, in Erfurt, deploys a force of the same size. Frontier Command Centre has an artillery regiment, six static and one 'crossing point' Frontier Troop regiments, and provides the security forces surrounding Berlin. There are two independent Frontier Troop regiments on the Polish and Czechoslovak border. According to some sources, in 1979 these units began to be reconfigured into special motor rifle divisions, but full details are as yet unknown.

The Frontier Regiments are trained as infantry and consist of about 1,500 men in three battalions, each with four companies. Most units are more lightly armed than normal NVA units, their heaviest weapons being RPG-7s. The exceptions are the regiments of Frontier Command Centre, which are mechanised. These are based around four rifle companies each with three platoons riding PSzH-IV or FUG armoured vehicles, and a fourth dismounted platoon. These regiments also have an anti-tank gun battery and a mortar battery as well as an engineer company. The regiments are configured for incorporation into special motor rifle divisions in time of war.

A posting to the Frontier Troops provides a soldier with a better than average opportunity to escape from East Germany. For this reason, the

The East German NVA maintain one of the most extensive security organisations in the Warsaw Pact. Among these units are the heavily militarised Grenzschutz, the direct counterpart of the Soviet KGB Border Guard units. (Eastfoto)

Below
The Czechoslovak 22nd Abn. Regt. makes extensive use of the locally manufactured M-59A 82 mm recoilless rifle for fire support.

Men of the 22nd Abn. Regt. prepare their light trucks for airdrop during an exercise in 1980—note that the older pattern camouflage clothing, phased out of use by much of the rest of the Czech Army, is still worn here. (Eastfoto)

Paratroopers of the Czechoslovak 22nd Airborne Regt. during field exercises. Note Skorpion machine pistol; parachute canopy in drab camouflage; and drab grey-brown field beret, which replaces the red type when 'tactical'.

political reliability of inductees is a primary concern. It is not a particularly popular posting in the German armed forces, since it requires personnel willing to fire on fleeing citizens, and soldiers are subject to particularly strict discipline.

The élite of the German internal security forces is the *Felix Dzerzhinsky Wach Regiment der MfS*. This Guard Regiment is subordinated to the Ministry of State Security and is controlled by the MfS, the German equivalent of the KGB. It is responsible for internal security activities and the guarding of key governmental facilities. It would also appear to have significant military and commando functions, as elements of it are parachute-qualified. Although called a regiment, it is in fact a fairly large force, numbering about 7,100 troops. It is organised around three command groups, two of which consist of three motor rifle battalions using the PSzH-IV or BTR-60PB armoured troop carriers. The third command group consists of training battalions. The regiment is provided with a scout company, signal company and an engineer battalion and has an organic helicopter squadron with six Mi-2, six Mi-8 and six Mi-24 Hind D helicopters.

Czechoslovakia

The CSLA (*Ceskoslovenska lidova armada:* Czechoslovak People's Army) deploys a fairly small number of élite troops. The 1968 invasion of Czechoslovakia was followed by a purge of the Army, which resulted in widespread demoralisation and difficulty in filling officer and NCO positions with competent, motivated personnel. Prior to the invasion the CSLA had an airborne brigade, the *22 Vysadkova Brigada*; but this unit is currently reduced to regimental size, possibly due to the aftermath of the events of 1968. It is stationed near Prosnice, and consists of one active, one reserve, one special operations and one training battalion plus support units. It has paraded with OT-64 SKOT armoured troop carriers, but when deployed on Warsaw Pact manoeuvres it does not appear to be very heavily mechanised. Like the East German airborne units, it appears to be a light airborne infantry force. There are also reports that the CSLA has a commando battalion, but details are lacking. There are also references to a 7th Airborne Battalion, but again, few details are available. In contrast to the East German and Polish armies, the Czechoslovak border guards (PS) are under Ministry of the Interior control, as are the Interior Guards (VS).

The uniform of Romanian mountain infantry retains characteristic features from the Second World War period, including the large beret.

Hungary

The Hungarian People's Army has only a single airborne battalion, 400 men strong. Hungary had an airborne division based at Taszar until 1956, but it was apparently disbanded after the 1956 Hungarian Uprising and the subsequent subordination of the Army to the Warsaw Pact's firm control. As in the case of Czechoslovakia, both the Interior Guard and Frontier Guards are a part of the Ministry of the Interior rather than the armed forces.

Romania

The Army of the Romanian Socialist Republic deploys a single airborne regiment, two mountain infantry brigades and a naval infantry battalion. Although nominally a member of the Warsaw Pact, the ARSR does not participate to any extent in Warsaw Pact manoeuvres beyond representation by observers. The Romanian Army of the Second World War formed the 1st Paratroop Battalion, but this was later disbanded. The ARSR currently has a single airborne unit, the 161st Paratroop Regiment, based at Buzau. Very little is known of its organisation, but it is believed to be a relatively lightly equipped unit. Romanian mountain units represent a traditional branch of the infantry, and were well represented in the Romanian Army of the Second World War. After the war Romania still maintained three mountain divisions; but with the advent of mechanisation these were gradually converted to motor rifle divisions along Soviet lines. All that remains today are two brigades, the 2nd Mountain Brigade in Brasov and the 4th Mountain Brigade at Curtea de Arges, which are believed to be organised on the basis of two mountain infantry regiments each. The Romanian Navy has a single naval infantry battalion stationed at Giurgia, but this is a coast defence unit rather than a naval landing force. Separate from the Army is a 17,000-man Frontier Troops force, and a 20,000-strong Security Troops force subordinated to the Ministry of Internal Affairs.

Bulgaria

The Bulgarian People's Army deploys a modest force of élite units. It had deployed mountain infantry brigades until 1958, when they were mostly converted to motor rifle units. However, in recent years at least one of these units has reverted to specialisation in mountain warfare. The Bulgarian People's Army formed its first airborne units around 1948, and currently have a single regiment which is based in the Burgas-Plovdiv region. There are reportedly a number of Bulgarian specialist commando units, but no details are known. The Bulgarian Navy has three Naval Guard companies, which appear to be shore defence units rather than marine landing groups, but which have participated with Soviet Naval Infantry in amphibious landing exercises on Bulgaria's Black Sea coast.

The Bulgarian Navy deploys about three companies of Naval Infantry, which have trained for amphibious operations alongside Soviet troops during exercises in the Black Sea. In combat the Naval Infantry—seen here on parade—wear the normal Bulgarian steel helmet, but painted light blue and with a prominent red star on the front. (Eastfoto)

TABLE 1: ORGANISATION AND EQUIPMENT **Soviet Air Assault Division**

	Troops	BMD-2 KSh Command AFV	BMD-2 Support AFV	BMD-1 Airborne AFV	BRDM-2 ATGM AFV	BRDM-2 Scout AFV	ASU-85 assault gun AFV	D-30 122 mm howitzer	RPU-14 140 mm MRL	120 mm mortar	SA-7 Grail AA launcher	ZU-23 23 mm AA gun	RPG-7D/RPG-16D AT	AGS-17 grenade launcher	RPKS 5-45 mm lmg	Trucks and vehicles	Trailers	Radios
Div. HQ	160	3			2						6		6	4		33	9	16
Air Assault Regts. (3)	4365	30	27	270	27	12				18	108	18	333	54	249	672	135	693
Artillery Regt.	620							30	6		21		40		36	124	37	60
Assault Gun Bn.	180						31				12		2			11	7	35
Air Defence Bn.	155										12	18				26		11
Engineer Bn.	220										6		12			45	4	9
Signal Bn.	180										6		11	4		21	6	14
Reconnaissance Co.	75					9					6		9		8	3		10
Support Units*	545										6		8			272	7	10

*Support units include a parachute rigging and resupply battalion, a transport and maintenance battalion, a medical battalion and a chemical defence battalion.

The Plates

Since Soviet and Warsaw Pact élite units generally wear uniforms basically similar to those of the rest of their armies, we have concentrated in these plates mainly upon those items of dress, insignia and equipment which are peculiar to the specific branches of service covered in this book.

A1: Paratrooper, Soviet VDV; summer jump uniform, early 1980s

The basic uniform is a field drab coverall (*kombinezon*) which is peculiar to the VDV. The VDV emblem is evident on the sleeves, but no rank insignia are worn. The leather helmet is derived from the standard VVS helicopter crew helmet; it is currently in the process of replacement by a new type modelled on the winter jump helmet, but unlined and in olive green material. The parachute is the standard D-5, with Z-5 ventral reserve; this rig is used both for training and for combat, with a brightly coloured canopy in the training mode.

TABLE 2: ORGANISATION AND EQUIPMENT
Soviet Air Assault Brigade*

	Troops	BMD-1 AFV	BRDM-2 Scout AFV	BRDM-3/AT-5 Spandrel	SA-7 Grail AA missile launcher	ZU-23 23 mm AA gun	120 mm mortar	AT-4 Spigot launcher	SPG-9 recoilless rifle	SD-44 85 mm AT gun (sp)	RPG-7 AT rocket launcher	AGS-17 grenade launcher
Brigade HQ	80				3						3	
Assault Bns. (2)	600	64			18		6				64	12
Airborne Bns. (2)	600				18			14	36		64	12
Reconnaissance Co.	75		4								3	
Air Defence Bty.	35				3	6						
Engineer Co.	55											
Signals Co.	60											
Artillery Bn.	205				3					6	6	
Anti-tank Bty.	60			9								2
Parachute Rigging Co.	70											
Transport Co.	70											
Chemical Defence Ptn.	10											
Medical Co.	25											
Supply Co.	30											

*Provisional data

TABLE 3: ORGANISATION AND EQUIPMENT
Soviet Air Mobile Brigade*

	Troops	120 mm mortar	SA-7 Grail AA missile	ZU-23 23 mm AA gun	BRDM-3/AT-5 Spandrel	AT-4 Spigot ATGM launcher	SPG-9 recoilless rifle	SD-44 85 mm AT gun (sp)	AGS-17 grenade launcher	BRDM-2 Scout AFV
Brigade HQ	80		3							
Airborne Bns. (3)	750		27			21	54		12	
Heavy Bn.	275		3			7	18		6	
Reconnaissance Co.	75									4
Air Defence Bty.	35		3	6						
Engineer Co.	55									
Engineer Co.										
Signals Co.	60									
Mortar Bty.	62	6								
Anti-Tank Gun Bty.	60							6		
Anti-Tank Bty.	60				9					
Transport Co.	70									
Chemical Defence Ptn.	10									
Medical Co.	25									
Supply Co.	30									

A2: Paratrooper, Soviet VDV; winter jump uniform, early 1980s

The winter gear includes a lined jacket, with a collar of synthetic fur ('fish fur'). Various headgear can be worn on the drop, including the normal Ground Forces pile *ushanka*; but the ribbed helmet is preferred for its protective features. It is derived from the winter tank crew helmet, but without earphones. Soviet paratroopers usually jump with the AKD assault rifle and a few magazines tucked behind the Z-5 ventral reserve pack.

A3: Soviet VDV Air Assault Division sleeve patch
A4: Variation—Air Assault Brigade patch (provisional)

B1: Paratrooper, Soviet VDV; summer combat dress, early 1980s

The VDV has been using increasingly the camouflage coveralls (*kamuflirovanniy letniy maskirovochniy kombinezon*). These are a standard style adopted by the Ground Forces in the 1970s; the one-piece coverall is the norm, but other cuts are available in the same material. Under this can be seen the striped shirt, traditional for Soviet naval élite units since the days of the Bolshevik Revolution, and owing its adoption by the VDV to the appointment of Maj. Gen. Margelov as VDV commander in the 1950s: Margelov had been in the Naval Infantry in the Second World War, and

TABLE 4: ORGANISATION AND EQUIPMENT
Soviet Naval Infantry Regiment

	Troops	BTR-60 AFV	PT-76 tank	T-55 tank	BRDM-2 AFV	ZSU-23-4 AA AFV	BRDM-2/SA-9 Gaskin	BM-21 Grad-P MRL	120 mm mortar	RPG-7	SA-7 AA missile launcher	SPG-9 recoilless rifle	AT-4 Spigot launcher	K-61 amphibian vehicle
Regimental HQ	60	4												
Naval Infantry Bns. (3)	1227	102							9	81	27	9	9	
Tank Bn.	188	3	31	10										
Reconnaissance Co.	50		3		9	4	4							
Anti-Tank Bty.	30											6		
Multiple Rocket Bty.	66							6						
Air Defence Bty.	58													
Engineer Co.	70													3
Signal Co.	57	2												
Chemical Defence Co.	36				3									
Transportation Co.	74													
Supply Co.	39													
Maintenance Co.	57													
Medical Co.	27													

TABLE 5: ORGANISATION AND EQUIPMENT
Polish 6th Pomeranian Air Assault Division*

	Troops	OT-64 SKOT AFV	BMP-1 AFV	BRDM-2 ATGM AFV	BRDM-2 Scout AFV	BRDM-2/SA-9 Gaskin	RPG-7D AT rocket	WP-8 140 mm MRL	D-30 122 mm howitzer	120 mm mortar	ZU-2 23 mm AA gun	SA-7 AA missile launcher
Div. HQ	100						6					6
Airborne Regts. (3)	3100	23	12				230			12		95
Artillery Bn.	240							12	6	12		12
Air Defence Bn.	135					4					18	12
Anti-Tank Bty.	45			9			9					
Transport Bn.	165						12					6
Engineer Co.	65						4					12
Signals Bn.	120				4		4					6
Reconnaissance Co.	60				4		8					6
Support Units**	350				3		8					6

*Data on this unit is very sketchy and this chart should be regarded as provisional
**Support units include a parachute rigging company, a medical company and chemical defence battalion

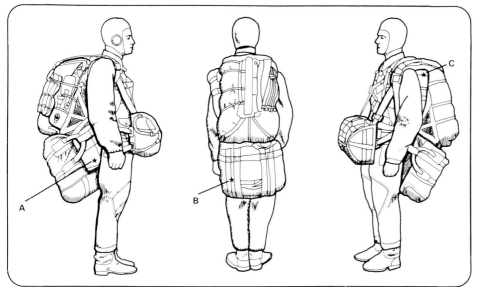

During combat jumps, Soviet paratroopers also add their rucksack and a special weapons bag under the dorsal 'chute pack. The weapons bag is released after leaving the aircraft, to dangle on a tether about 15 ft below the paratrooper. A rifle case is currently rigged behind the left shoulder (A) Rucksack (B) weapons bag (C) rifle case.

ordered the shirt to emphasise the élite nature of the VDV. In the 1960s the VDV wore a red beret, like most Western paratroop formations; but subsequently changed to this pale blue headgear, in keeping with the traditionally close ties with the VVS—Air Force. The SVD sniper's rifle reminds us that such weapons are distributed to a far greater extent within Soviet formations than is the case in comparable Western formations.

B2: Soviet 'Spetsnaz' in KGB Border Guards uniform, early 1980s

The *Spetsnaz* units do not have their own uniforms, but adopt standard Soviet uniforms as the occasion warrants. This particular soldier wears an outfit typical of those worn by the Border Guards in the current fighting in Afghanistan: the camouflage coveralls, with the tropical field hat issued to Border Guards and Ground Forces units in Central Asia and the Soviet Far East, where summer temperatures are extremely high. As well as the silenced AKS, he carries an RPG-18 rocket launcher, which is popular for general fire support as well as for anti-tank use.

B3: Soviet Mountain Infantryman, early 1980s

Among several items of clothing and equipment peculiar to the Mountain Infantry units, this dark

This official photo shows the service dress adopted by the VDV in the 1960s. It is of a lighter olive/khaki shade than that of the rest of the Army, and bears distinctions in pale blue, reflecting the traditional link with the Soviet Air Force. The striped sailor shirt was introduced in the 1950s by Gen. Margelov, a Second World War veteran of the Naval Infantry. (Sovfoto)

field drab coverall is immediately noticeable; it has lengths of elastic sewn into the fabric to hold the leggings close. Some Soviet troops in Afghanistan have been painting their helmets with sand-coloured camouflage blotches, as here. These troops are issued a rather rare commodity in the Soviet Union—sunglasses.

C1: Officer, Soviet VDV armoured unit, early 1980s

He wears the normal garrison working dress of VDV officers assigned to BMD units. The tank crew coveralls have the distinctive chest patch of the Armoured Forces; but the VDV's distinctive service dress cap, derived from the Air Force cap (and known by the slang term 'SS cap' for its high front), clearly identifies this officer's exact branch of service. He is armed with the AKR sub-machine gun, which is now becoming a standard personal weapon for armoured vehicle crews.

VDV paratroopers are presented with watches by the commander of the Air Assault Forces, Army Gen. D. Sukhorukov, during a ceremony in 1984. They wear a new pattern of uniform which more closely resembles that of other Warsaw Pact forces—note the shoulder pocket. (Sovfoto)

C2: Paratrooper, Soviet VDV; field service dress, early 1980s

The normal field service dress consists of the drab coverall shown on Plate A; but for day-to-day working wear, the Soviet paratrooper embellishes it with his distinctive emblems—the Russian soldier has traditionally worn his decorations even in battle. Today there are many varieties: Guards unit badges, specialist and parachute qualification badges, even DOSAAF parachute badges. This soldier is armed with an AKD assault rifle; this is a special version of the AKS-74 with a sideways-folding stock for airborne use. It is fitted with the new BG-15 40 mm grenade launcher.

C3: KGB Border Guard, field service dress, early 1980s

The Border Guards have traditionally relied upon the Ground Forces for their uniforms. However, in the early 1980s they were the first to introduce this new uniform (*kamuflirovanniy kurtki*) which combines the standard Soviet camouflage fabric with a more traditional 'service dress' cut. The Border Guards shoulder boards and collar tabs are of normal Ground Forces style, but in their distinctive green

colour; the Cyrillic lettering on the shoulder boards is 'PV' for Border Guards, and 'VV' for the Interior Army. The normal service dress cap also displays the green branch-of-service colour.

D1: Soviet Naval Infantryman, combat dress, 1975

This figure displays the older pattern of Soviet camouflage coveralls, which have been in use since the 1960s; this is still to be seen, in dwindling numbers, particularly among Soviet Naval Infantry and in some Warsaw Pact armies. The standard SSh-60 steel helmet has an outline red star on the front—a common Naval Infantry practice—and an anchor insignia on the side.

D2: Soviet Naval Infantryman, combat dress, 1985

Like the Ground Forces and the VDV, the Naval Infantry have been adopting the new-pattern camouflage clothing since the 1970s. This soldier wears the Naval Infantry's black beret; compare this enlisted ranks' cap badge with the slightly different officers' pattern shown on E1, and note that the red-pennant-and-gold-anchor badge is worn on both sides of the beret. The weapon illustrated is the 9P54M, which fires the 9M32M Strela II anti-aircraft missile—'SA-7 Grail' in NATO parlance. When the missile is fired the whole tube assembly is disposable, leaving only the lower firing gripstock, which is carried in this special canvas holster.

D3: Soviet Naval Infantry sleeve patch

E1: Captain 2nd Rank, Soviet Naval Infantry; summer field service dress, 1985

This uniform is patterned after the Ground Forces style, but in black rather than olive drab material. The distinctive blue and white striped shirt is worn by all ranks with field dress. The field quality shoulder boards, in black with red braid, identify the exact rank by the number of stripes and stars. The sleeve badge is the branch insignia of the Naval Infantry—other elements of the Soviet Navy wear similar badges of various designs. This officer is armed with an APS Stechkin automatic pistol with a wooden holster-stock.

E2: Soviet Naval Infantryman, winter field dress, 1985

Again, a direct copy of the Ground Forces

Naval Infantry of the Black Sea Fleet in winter combat dress. In naval service the standard Soviet Army SSh-60 steel helmet is often emblazoned with an outline red star on the front, just visible here under the camouflage netting. (Sovfoto)

equivalent uniform, but in black. The shoulder boards display the Cyrillic 'BF' identifying the Baltic Fleet Naval Infantry Regiment; the single stripe indicates the rank of senior seaman. As well as the red outline star, the helmet bears a painted version of the Naval Infantry pennant. He is armed with the RPKS (RPK-74), the new version of the standard RPK squad automatic weapon.

E3: Soviet Naval Infantry tank crewman, 1985

Armoured vehicle crews of the Naval Infantry wear dark blue coveralls of similar cut to the Ground Forces equivalent, with the distinctive striped shirt. This soldier is identified as a vehicle commander, and therefore a sergeant, by the numbers stencilled on his coveralls: '532-1', i.e. commander of vehicle turret number '532'. Commanders carry a set of flags for signalling to other vehicles during periods of radio silence. He wears the normal Naval Infantry beret and cap badge.

F1: Paratrooper, Polish 6 PDPD; jump uniform, 1970

The Polish 6th Pomeranian Air Assault Division (6 PDPD) wear uniforms virtually identical to those of the rest of the Polish Army. This man wears the old-pattern field uniform, which had splinter-pattern camouflage patches as well as the more common 'rain-drop' scheme: one of several varieties of camouflage pattern used by the Poles, and similar to materials which have also been employed by the Czechs and Bulgarians. The old-pattern jump headgear had folding ear-pieces. The shoulder emblem is one of several similar geometric shapes worn within the 6 PDPD; their significance is not certain, but they may have been battalion patches.

The parachute is the Polish version of the Soviet D-3, with Z-1P ventral reserve.

F2: Paratroop officer, Polish 6 PDPD; summer field service dress, 1985

This senior lieutenant in the current field service uniform wears the 6 PDPD's red beret. It was selected in 1963 under the astonishingly mistaken impression that the Polish Airborne Brigade of the Second World War had worn the British paratrooper's maroon headgear—in fact, of course, the Poles wore pale blue-grey. The silver braid Piast eagle, the current Polish national emblem, is worn centrally on the beret, above rank insignia; this latter is repeated on the shoulder straps[1]. The Parachute Instructor's Badge is worn above the right breast pocket. He is armed with the PM 63 machine pistol, and wears its holster and pouch.

([1]*Erratum*—braid shoulder strap edging is shown in error and should be ignored.)

An interesting group of Naval Infantry in the black field service uniform. Both the lieutenant-colonel in the foreground and the petty officer behind his right shoulder wear parachute qualification badges—an increasing number of Soviet Naval Infantry personnel are being jump-trained. (Sovfoto)

F3: Paratrooper, Polish 6 PDPD; winter combat dress, 1985

The Polish Army's standard winter field jacket comes in both camouflage and plain olive drab patterns. On his shoulder this man displays the current formation patch of the 6 PDPD. The current red and white divisional patch is complemented by about 15 other colour variations which may be used to distinguish companies. The padded paratrooper's helmet is one of the few distinctive elements of the division's field dress, and is worn only by the 6 PDPD and the Podhale WOP Mountain Brigade. He carries the PKM light machine gun, which is used to provide supporting fire at longer range than the lighter RPK squad automatic.

F4: Current 6 PDPD divisional shoulder patch

F5: Unidentified unit shoulder patch, within 6 PDPD, 1970s

G1: Warrant officer, Polish 7 LDDM; summer field service dress, 1970s–80s

This junior WO wears the standard field uniform of the Army, as the 7th Luzycka Naval Assault Division—although the closest Warsaw Pact equivalent to the US Marines—is in fact an Army formation and not part of the Polish Navy. The distinctive uniform items are the blue beret and divisional shoulder patch.

G2: Naval Assault Infantryman, Polish 7 LDDM; winter combat dress, 1985

This uniform is essentially similar to that of the rest of the Army, apart from the divisional shoulder patch. The steel helmet has a cloth cover instead of the more usual netting; there are small loops for attaching foliage camouflage, and an embroidered Polish eagle badge on the front. The weapon shown here is the PMK-DGN-60, a Polish derivative of the AKM capable of launching a range of grenades— this example is an anti-tank grenade.

G3: Mountain Infantryman, Polish Podhale WOP Mountain Brigade; service dress, 1985

The Podhale Brigade retains the distinctive and traditional service and walking-out uniform of Polish mountain infantry from the period 1920–39. The hat and cape, based on the folk costume of the

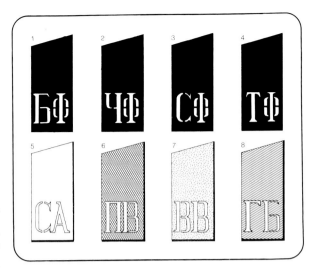

Soviet Naval Infantry shoulder boards—black with yellow lettering, for enlisted men only: (1) Baltic Fleet (2) Black Sea Fleet (3) Northern Fleet (4) Pacific Fleet. Shoulder boards of (5) Soviet Army—pale blue with yellow lettering for VDV paratroops; (6) Border Guards—yellow lettering on green; (7) Interior Army—yellow lettering on dark red; and (8) KGB Special Units—yellow lettering on royal blue.

Podhale region of the Polish Carpathian mountains, are peculiar to this unit. The edelweiss emblem is a new addition, however: the old mountain infantry insignia of the pre-1939 period incorporated a short-armed swastika in their design. The field dress of this unit is conventional, differing from standard Polish infantry patterns only in the use of the padded paratrooper-style helmet.

G4: Polish 7 LDDM divisional shoulder patch

G5: Polish Podhale WOP Mountain Brigade shoulder patch

H1: Paratroop officer, Czechoslovak 22nd Airborne Regiment; field service dress, 1980

This paratroop officer wears 1965-pattern Czechoslovak camouflaged field uniform—in fact, the standard camouflage uniform for the whole Army, although often wrongly identified as 'airborne camouflage dress'. Although still seen in use as late as 1980, this pattern has been gradually phased out of service. Distinctive features identifying the 22nd Airborne Regiment are the red beret, with its lion cap badge, and the regimental patch on the upper sleeve. In the field, the red beret gives way to a less conspicuous dark grey-brown beret. The Czechoslovak Army wear rank insignia above the right breast pocket of field uniform, and this figure displays the single gold star between two lines of braid which indicates a sub-lieutenant. On service dress ranking is worn on the shoulder boards, with a silver arm-of-service insignia. The weapon is the Skorpion machine pistol.

H2: Paratrooper, Czechoslovak 22nd Airborne Regiment; summer combat dress, 1985

Contemporary Czechoslovak field dress is not significantly different from those of the other Warsaw Pact armies, although Czech uniforms tend to be of a slightly greyer background shade, Polish uniforms slightly greener, and German slightly browner. The two steel pips over the right breast pocket identify this soldier as a corporal. He wears the Czechoslovak paratrooper helmet; and is armed with the vz.58, a variation on the AKM.

H3: Czechoslovak 22nd Airborne Regiment sleeve patch
H4: Czechoslovak airborne troops' arm-of-service insignia
H5: Vehicle marking, Czechoslovak 22nd Airborne Regiment

I1: Unterfeldwebel, NVA 40th Airborne Battalion; winter walking-out uniform, 1985

The walking-out dress of the East German airborne battalions is essentially similar to that of the rest of the GDR's army; and in many respects it recalls German military traditions of an earlier generation. The arm-of-service colour is bright orange-red, displayed not only at collar, shoulder and cuff but also as a beret—for enlisted ranks bearing a small gold, black and red version of the GDR's national emblem, and for officers the same badge partly enclosed by silver oak leaves. (The orange beret was, supposedly, selected in preference to the usual maroon to commemorate the colour of a cap worn during the 15th century peasant rebellions in Germany.) The collar patches are orange, and bear silver-grey parachute-and-wing devices; they are edged in silver for officers. The traditional *Tresse* braid edging is worn on the collar by NCO ranks; and the shoulder straps indicate rank, NCO status, and arm-of-service in exactly the same way as the old *Wehrmacht* shoulder straps, though in cheaper modern materials. This enlisted man wears a line of silver-grey piping round the top of the cuff; and two plain silver-grey *Litzen* bars on the cuff, with orange central 'lights'—officers have the same piping, but

A scout patrol of the 7th Luzycka Naval Assault Div. on exercise near Poland's Baltic coast. The uniform is distinguishable from that of the rest of the Army only by the blue service dress beret, and the divisional shoulder patch, just visible here on the winter combat jacket: see Plate G.

fancier *Litzen*. The parachute emblem on the left forearm is the distinctive insignia of the airborne troops.

I2, I3: Paratroopers, NVA 40th Airborne Battalion; summer combat dress, 1985

Apart from the special paratrooper's helmet, and knitted details at neck and wrist, the only distinctive feature identifying the NVA airborne soldier is the grey-brown field beret, which substitutes for the excessively conspicuous orange headgear when troops are 'tactical'. Although I2 wears the standard Warsaw Pact RPG-7 grenade backpack, note that he carries the interesting RPG-7D variant, which can be disassembled into two parts to shorten the launch tube for the convenience of paratroopers.

J1: Bulgarian paratrooper, combat dress, 1980s

The Bulgarian Army employs a multi-colour 'splinter/rain-drop' camouflage pattern; there are a number of different field uniforms, but that worn by this paratrooper is essentially similar to that of the rest of the army. Bulgarian airborne troops wear a brown leather helmet derived from that of the tank crews, but without earphones.

The Romanian 161st Parachute Regt. is the only major airborne unit of the ASRS. Like many of the smaller Warsaw Pact airborne elements, it lacks the substantial armoured vehicle assets of comparable Soviet units. Note the special paratrooper helmet, and the collar and shoulder insignia; two yellow stripes across the shoulder strap, piped pale blue, identify a paratroop corporal.

J2, J3: Bulgarian Mountain Infantrymen, summer field dress, 1985

The Bulgarian mountain infantry wear one of the more distinctive Warsaw Pact uniforms; it is notable for the extensive and unusual integral padding, and for the areas of black material—reinforcement, perhaps? Of fairly recent adoption, this uniform may be taken into use by the paratroopers. One of the unique features of the field uniform is the beret in camouflage material, worn with a tricolour national flash. The rappelling harness appears, from its colour, to be of commercial design.

K1: Paratrooper, Romanian 161st Parachute Regiment; summer jump uniform, 1980s

The current Romanian paratrooper's field uniform and jump gear; the helmet is of Romanian design. The pale blue arm-of-service colour is displayed on collar tabs of traditional Romanian shape. His weapon is the Romanian version of the AKM, which has a unique foregrip.

K2: Romanian Mountain Infantryman, summer field service dress, 1980s

The Romanian mountain infantry regiments retain the khaki drab beret traditional since the 1930s. The arm-of-service colour, dark green, is displayed on the collar tabs; and on the shoulder straps as edging to the transverse rank stripes in gold—two stripes identify a corporal. The arm-of-service insignia is pinned 'inboard' of the ranking. The special mountain boots, worn with turned-down socks, are peculiar to the mountain troops. This soldier carries the FPK, a derivative of the Soviet SVD sniper's rifle.

K3: Bulgarian airborne troops' arm-of-service insignia
K4: Vehicle marking, Romanian 161st Parachute Regt. (the arm-of-service insignia is the same, in bronze)
K5: Romanian mountain troops' arm-of-service insignia

L: Soviet Bloc élite forces insignia:
L1: East German combat swimmer insignia. *L2:* Soviet VDV vehicle insignia, Guards Air Assault Divisions. *L3:* Polish paratroop instructor's badge. *L4:* Polish paratrooper's qualification badge. *L5:* East German paratrooper's qualification badge. *L6:* Soviet paratrooper's qualification badge. *L7:* Soviet master paratrooper's badge. *L8:* Soviet paratroop instructor's badge. *L9:* Czechoslovak paratrooper's qualification badge. *L10:* Czechoslovak first class paratrooper's badge. *L11:* Czechoslovak master paratrooper's badge. *L12:* Czechoslovak paratroop instructor's badge.

One of the new Bulgarian mountain infantry units on exercise in 1984, wearing the latest multi-tone camouflage uniform and matching beret—see Plate J.

Order of Battle of the Soviet VDV Air Assault Force

Commander: Army General D. S. Sukhorukov
1st Deputy Commander: Lt. Gen. Y. Kurochkin
Chief of Staff: Lt. Gen. P. Pavlenko

6th Guards 'Kremenchug-Znamenka' Air Assault Division
(Far Eastern Military District; base, Belogorsk-Khabarovsk)
    14th Guards Air Assault Regiment
    17th Guards Air Assault Regiment
    20th Guards Air Assault Regiment
    8th Guards Air Assault Artillery Regiment

76th Guards 'Chernigov-Brest Litovsk-Kovel-Elnya' Air Aslt. Div.
(Leningrad MD; base, Pskov)
    234th Guards Air Aslt. Regt.
    237th Guards Air Aslt. Regt.
    239th Guards Air Aslt. Regt.
    154th Guards Air Aslt. Arty. Regt.

102nd Guards 'Svir-Petrozavodosk' Air Aslt. Div.
(Odessa MD; base, Kishniev)
    1061st Guards Air Aslt. Regt.
    1063rd Guards Air Aslt. Regt.
    1065th Guards Air Aslt. Regt.
    850th Guards Air Aslt. Arty. Regt.

103rd Guards Air Aslt. Div.
(Limited Contingent of Soviet Forces—Afghanistan; base, Kabul/Bagram)
    393rd Guards Air Aslt. Regt.
    583rd Guards Air Aslt. Regt.
    688th Guards Air Aslt. Regt.
    271st Guards Air Aslt. Arty. Regt.

104th Guards Air Aslt. Div.
(Transcaucasus MD; base, Kirovabad)
    217th Guards Air Aslt. Regt.
    242nd Guards Air Aslt. Regt.
    273rd Guards Air Aslt. Regt.
    290th Guards Air Aslt. Arty. Regt.

106th Guards 'Zabaikal-Dniepr' Air Aslt. Div.
(Moscow MD; base, Tula-Ryazan)
    43rd Guards Air Aslt. Regt.
    188th Guards Air Aslt. Regt.
    236th Guards Air Aslt. Regt.
    352nd Guards Air Aslt. Arty. Regt.

107th (7th?) Guards 'Cherkassy' Air Aslt. Div.
(Baltic MD; base, Kaunus)
    18th Guards Air Aslt. Regt.
    21st Guards Air Aslt. Regt.
    29th Guards Air Aslt. Regt.
    10th Guards Air Aslt. Arty. Regt.

(Left) The Polish paratrooper instructor's badge: see Plate L3. (Right) The Soviet paratrooper instructor's badge, with the 100-jump feature attached, and a supplementary tab hooked to the bottom to mark a further 25 jumps. This tab is marked '10' on one side and '25' on the other. See Plate L8.

Notes sur les planches en couleur

A1 Les insignes de combinaison et de manche permettre de reconnaître les VDV; le casque est dérivé du casque d'équipage d'hélicoptère; les parachutes sont le D-5 (dorsal) et le Z-5 (ventral). **A2** Notez l'addition de la veste d'hiver au col en fourrure synthétique—'fourrure de poisson'—et le casque doublé, basé sur le modèle de l'équipage de char. Le fusil AKD et des chargeurs sont poussés derrière le parachute ventral. **A3, A4** Insignes de manche des Divisions et des Brigades d'assaut aérien VDV, respectivement.

Farbtafeln

A1 Die Abzeichen auf dem Overall und den Ärmeln identifizieren die VDV; der Helm basiert auf dem Helm für Hubschrauberbesatzungsmitglieder; Die Fallschirme sind die Modelle D-5 und Z-5. **A2** Man beachte die zusätzliche Winterjacke mit synthetischem Pelzkragen und den gefütterten Helm (nach dem Helm für Panzerbesatzungsmitglieder). Das AKD Gewehr und einige Magazine werden hinter den Bodenfallschirm geworfen. **A3, A4** Ärmelabzeichen für die Luftangriffsdivisionen bzw. -brigaden der VDV.

B1 La combinaison camouflée apparut pour la première fois dans les années 1970; la chemise rayée de marin dans les années 1950, lorsqu'un ex-membre de l'Infanterie Navale commandait les VDV. Le béret bleu clair remplaça un béret rouge à la fin des années 1960. **B2** Les 'Spetsnaz' n'ont pas d'uniforme particulier mais ils portent l'uniforme de l'unité dans laquelle ils servent; ici, une combinaison camouflée et un chapeau tropical, portés durant l'été afghan par les Gardes de Frontière. Il porte un AKS à silencieux et un RPG-18. **B3** Notez le casque camouflé, habituel en Afghanistan et les jambes en tissu élastique de la combinaison spéciale.

C1 Son chapeau, similaire à celui de l'Armée de l'Air, indique que cet officier est un parachutiste, en dépit de la combinaison de troupe blindée qu'il porte pour service dans une unité BMD. Il porte un AKR. **C2** Tenue de travail quotidienne, la combinaison de parachutiste est embellie avec des insignes et des décorations. Notez le fusil AKD équipé du nouveau lance-grenades de 20 mm. **C3** Cet uniforme de camouflage taillé comme une tenue de service conventionnelle fut lancé par les Gardes de Frontière du KGB au début des années 1980; notez les insignes verts du KGB, etc.

D1 La combinaison de camouflage plus ancienne des années 1960, encore vue en petit nombre dans les unités de l'Infanterie Navale. Notez les insignes de casque à étoile et ancre. **D2** Le béret noir de l'Infanterie Navale, porté avec des insignes à banderole des deux côtés, vu ici avec la nouvelle tenue de camouflage. Le mécanisme de tir du missile Strela II, conservé lorsque le tube de lancement déployé est jeté, est porté dans l'étui illustré. **D3** Insigne de manche de l'Infanterie Navale.

E1 Coupé comme l'uniforme kaki de l'armée, mais en noir, avec insignes de l'Infanterie Navale (notez l'insigne de chapeau de l'officier). Le grade est indiqué par des galons rouges et des étoiles dorées sur des épaulettes noires. L'arme est le pistolet Stechkin APS, avec étui/monture combinés en bois. **E2** Les pattes d'épaule portent 'BF' en lettres cyrilliques, permettant de reconnaître le régiment d'infanterie navale de la flotte de la Baltique. Le galon unique indique le grade de matelot breveté. Il porte la mitraillette légère RPKS. **E3** Le numéro '532-1' indique le sergent commandant du char N° 532. Les drapeaux de signalisation sont utilisés durant les périodes de silence de radio. Le béret est le même que celui de l'Infanterie Navale.

F1 Le camouflage de dessin 'éclat' et 'goutte de pluie' combiné fut utilisé dans les années 1970. Les insignes d'épaule sont peut-être celles d'un bataillon de la 6ème Division d'assaut aérien. **F2** Uniforme de camouflage actuel, le béret rouge de parachutiste portant l'aigle polonais et l'insigne de grade, ce dernier étant répété sur l'épaule. Notez le pistolet automatique PM 63 et son étui et cartouchière. **F3** Tenue de combat d'hiver, avec casque de parachutiste rembourré et mitraillette PKM. **F4** Insignes d'épaule actuels de la 6ème Division. **F5** Insigne de bataillon non identifié, 1970.

G1, G2 A part le béret bleu et les insignes d'épaule, la 7ème Division d'assaut naval porte l'uniforme de l'armée. Notez l'insigne à aigle sur le revêtement en toile du casque porté par G2, qui porte la variante PMK-DGN-60 de l'AKM, muni d'une grenade anti-char. **G3** A part l'insigne à edelweiss remplaçant les swastikas d'avant-guerre et un col ouvert moderne, cet uniforme est pratiquement le même que la tenue carpathienne traditionnelle des troupes de montagne de 1939. **G4, G5** Insignes d'épaule de la 7ème Division et de la Brigade de montagne, respectivement.

H1 Cette tenue de camouflage fut portée par l'armée tchèque de 1965 à 1980 quoique qu'elle soit actuellement démodée. Le béret rouge à l'insigne national de lion et les insignes de manche permettent de reconnaître le 22ème Régiment aéroporté et un insigne de grade de sous-lieutenant est porté sur le sein droit. Notez le pistolet automatique Skorpion. **H2** Uniforme de camouflage actuel de parachutiste tchèque, avec casque de fabrication tchèque, insigne de grade de caporal sur le sein droit et fusil vz 58. **H3** Insigne de manche du 22ème Régiment aéroporté. **H4** Insigne des troupes aéroportées tchèques. **H5** Marquage de véhicule, 22ème Régiment.

I1 Tenue de sortie NVA standard, avec béret orange, écussons, et ganse d'épaule des unités aéroportées; insigne d'avant-bras gauche de parachutiste. **I2, I3** Les caractéristiques spéciales de l'uniforme de parachutiste NVA sont: le casque, le col et les manchettes en tricot, le béret marron porté au lieu du type orange trop visible sur le terrain, le RPG-7D qui peut être divisé en deux pour le rendre plus court et plus commode.

J Davers codèles de tef5- de terrain sont u4alisés par les Bulgares dans ce dessin de camouflage 'éclat et goutte de pluie'. La version rembourrée et renforcée, portée avec un béret du même tissu, est propre aux troupes de montagne. Notez le harnais de rappel, qui d'après sa couleur vive est un article produit commercialement.

K1 Le bleu clair permet de reconnaitre les unités parachutistes et il est porté sur des pinces de col de forme roumaine traditonnelle. Le modèle local de l'AKM est reconnaissable à sa prise avant. **K2** Béret, bottes et distinctions vert foncé caractéristiques des troupes de montagne roumaines. Notez les galons de caporal sur les épaules et l'insigne des troupes de montagne; fusil de tirailleur FPK. **K3-5** Insigne des parachutistes bulgares; véhicule des parachutistes roumains; troupes de montagne roumaines.

L1 Insigne de nageur de combat de l'Allemagne de l'est. **L2** Insigne de véhicule, Division d'assaut aérien des gardes VDV. **L3, L4** Insignes de qualification de parachutiste et d'instructeur de parachutistes polonais. **L5, L6** Insignes de qualification des parachutistes soviétiques et de l'Allemagne de l'est. **L7, L8** Insignes de maître-parachutiste et d'instructeur de parachutistes soviétiques. **L9-12** Insignes de parachutiste qualifié, de parachutiste première classe, de maître-parachutiste et d'instructeur tchèques.

B1 Der Tarnoverall wurde erstmals in den 1970er Jahren benutzt, das gestreifte Matrosenhemd in den 1950ern, als ein früheres Mitglied der Marine-Infanterie den Oberbefehl der VDV übernahm. Ende der 1960er Jahre wurde das rote Barrett durch dieses blaue ersetzt. **B2** Die 'Spetsnaz' haben keine eigene Uniform, sondern tragen die Bekleidung der Einheiten, denen sie zugeordnet sind, hier Tarnoveralls und ein Tropenhelm, wie von den Grenzwächtern im Sommer vor Afghanistan getragen. Dazu gedämpftes AKS und ein RPG-18. **B3** Man beachte den Tarnhelm, eine in Afghanistan durchgeführte Praxis, und die Elastikhosenbeine der Spezialoveralls.

C1 Die Mütze, ähnlich wie bei der Air Force, identifiziert diesen Offizier als Fallschirmspringer, trotz des Panzertruppenoveralls der BMD-Einheit, dem er dient. Er trägt ein AKR. **C2** Für die tägliche Arbeitsausrüstung sind die Overalls der Fallschirmspringer mit Abzeichen und Dekorationen verziert. Man beachte das AKD Gewehr mit einem neuen 30 mm Granatenwerfer. **C3** Diese wie ein konventioneller Dienstanzug geschneiderte Tarnuniform wurde in den früher 1980er Jahren zuerst von den KGB Grenzwächtern getragen; man beachte die grünen KGB Abzeichen usw.

D1 Die älteren Tarnoveralls aus den 1960er Jahren, immer noch in kleiner Mengen bei Einheiten der Marine-Infanterie benutzt; man beachte Stern und Anker-Abzeichen auf dem Helm. **D2** Das schwarze Barrett der Marine Infanterie mit Wimpelabzeichen auf beiden Seiten, hier mit neuerer Tarnbekleidung getragen. Der Abschussmechanismus für das Strela II Geschoss der erhalten bleibt, wenn das verlängerte Startrohr abgefallen ist, wird in den hier abgebildeten Futteral getragen. **D3** Ärmelabzeichen der Marine-Infanterie.

E1 Gemustert wie die Khakiuniform der Armee, aber in schwarz, mit der Abzeichen der Marine-Infanterie (man beachte das Mützenabzeichen des Offiziers) und roten Streifen auf goldenen Schulterschleifen als Rangabzeichen. Die Waffe ist die Stechkin APS Pistole mit kombiniertem hölzernen Pistolenhalter/Schulterstütze. **E2** Die Schulterschleifen tragen die Aufschrift BF in kyrillischen Buchstaben für das Infanterie-Regiment der baltischen Marine-Flotte, der Streifen ist das Rangabzeichen eines höheren Seeoffiziers. Die Waffe ist ein leichtes RPKS MG. **E3** Die Zahl '532-1' identifiziert den Sergeanten mit Oberbefehl über Panzer Nr. 532. Signalflaggen werden verwendet, wenn Funkstille angeordnet wurde. Das Barrett ist identisch mit dem für die Infanterie.

F1 Tarnung mit gemischtem 'splitter' und 'Regentropfen' Muster, in den 1970er Jahren benutzt. Die Schulterabzeichen gehören vielleicht zu einem Bataillon der 6. Luftangriffsdivision. **F2** Heutige Tarnuniform mit dem polnischen Adler und Ragnabzeichen (letztere auch auf den Schultern) auf dem roten Barrett der Fallschirmspringer. Man beachte die PM 63 Maschinenpistole und den dazugehörigen Halter und Patronenbeutel. **F3** Winterkampfuniform mit gestepptem Fallschirmspringerhelm und PKM MG. **F4** Heutige Schulterzeichen der 6. Division. **F5** Nicht identifiziertes Bataillonsabzeichen von 1970.

G1, G2 Abgesehen von dem blauen Barrett und den Schulterabzeichen trägt die 7. Marine-Angriffsdivision die Uniform der Armee. Man beachte das Adlerabzeichen auf dem Helm-Stoffbezug auf G2, sowie die PMK-DGN-60 Variante der AKM mit einer angebauten Panzerabwehrgrante. **G3** Abgesehen von den Edelweiss-Abzeichen anstelle der Hakenkreuze der Vorkriegszeit und einem modernen offenen Kragen ist diese Uniform weitgehend identisch mit den traditionellem karpathischer Modell der Bergtruppen von 1939. **G4, G5** Schulterabzeichen der 7. Division bzw. Bergbrigade.

H1 Diese heute überholte Tarnuniform wurde von der tschechischen Armee vor 1965-80 getragen. Das rote Barrett mit dem Löwen-Nationalzeichen und die Ärmelabzeichen identifizieren das 22. Luftregiment. Die Rangabzeichen eines Unterleutnants werden auf der rechten Brustseite getragen. Man beachte die 'skorpion' Maschinenpistole. **H2** Heutige tschechische Fallschirmspringer-Tarnuniform mit einem in der Tschechoslowakei hergestellten Helm, Korporalsabzeichen auf der rechten brustseite und einem vz.58 Gewehr. **H3** Abzeichen des 22. Luftregiments auf dem Ärmel. **H4** Abzeichen der tschechischen Luftlandetruppen. **H5** Fahrzeugkennzeichen des 22. Regiments.

I1 Standard NVA Ausgehuniform mit dem orangefarbenen Barrett, dem Kragenabzeichen und den Schulterklappenröhren der Luft-Branche sowie dem Abzeichen auf dem linken Vorderarm. **I2, I3** Spezielle Kennzeichen der Uniform der Fallschirmspringer sind der Helm, gestrickter Kragen und Manschetten, braunes Barrett anstelle der auffälligen orangefarbenen Kopfbedeckung, im Feld und die aus praktischen Gründen in zwei Teile zerlegbare RPG-7D.

J Bulgarien verwendet verschiedene Typen von Felduniform mit diesem 'splitter/Regentropfen' Tarnmuster. Die gesteppte, verstärkte Ausführung mit einem Barrett aus dem gleichen Material gehört zu den Bergeinheiten. Man beachte den Harnisch, angesichts der hellen Farbe vermutlich kommerziell hergestellt.

K1 Hellblau ist die Farbe der Fallschirmspringer und wird für die traditionellen rumänischen Kragenklappen getragen. Das landeigene Modell der AKM zeichnet sich durch seinen vorderen Griff aus. **K2** Barrett, Stiefel und dunkelgrüne Abzeichen identifizieren die rumänischen Gebirgstruppen. Man beachte die Korporalsstreifen auf den Schulterschleifen mit den Gebirgstruppenabzeichen und einem FPK Scharfschützengewehr. **K3-5** Abzeichen der bulgarischen Fallschirmspringer; Fahrzeuge rumänischer Fallschirmspringer; rumänische Gebirgssoldaten.

L1 Kampfschwimmer-Abzeichen der DDR. **L2** Fahrzeugabzeichen der der VDV Luftangriffswachen. **L3, L4** Abzeichen für Fallschirmspringer-Lehrer und qualifizierte Fallschirmspringer. **L5, L6** Qualifikationsabzeichen der Fallschirmspringer der DDR und der UdSSR. **L7, L8** Abzeichen für sowjetische Meisterfallschirmspringer und Fallschirmspringer-Lehrer. **L9-12** Abzeichen für qualifizierte tschechische Fallschirmspringer, Fallschirmspringer der 1. Klasse, Meisterfallschirmspringer und Lehrer.